my
parents
were
awesome

my parents were awesome

Before Fanny Packs and Minivans, They Were People Too

EDITED BY

eliot glazer

VILLARD TRADE PAPERBACKS
New York

A Villard Books Trade Paperback Original

Introduction and compilation copyright © 2011 by Eliot Glazer

Published in the United States by Villard Books,
an imprint of The Random House Publishing Group,
a division of Random House, Inc., New York.

VILLARD BOOKS and VILLARD and "V" CIRCLED Design
are registered trademarks of Random House, Inc.

LIBRARY OF CONGRESS CATALOGING-IN-PUBLICATION DATA

My parents were awesome : before fanny packs and minivans,
they were people too / edited by Eliot Glazer.
p. cm.
ISBN 978-0-345-52392-1 (pbk.)
eBook ISBN 978-0-345-52818-6
1. Parents.   2. Parent and child.   3. Parent and adult child.
I. Glazer, Eliot.
HQ755.8.M92 2010
306.874092'2—dc22   2010034586

Printed in the United States of America

www.villard.com

9 8 7 6 5 4 3 2 1

Book design by Debbie Glasserman

Half-title photo: courtesy of Whitney Jefferson
Frontispiece photos: (top to bottom) courtesy of Lindsey
Weber; courtesy of Kyle Supley; courtesy of David Weiss;
courtesy of Steve Ponzo

For Mom and Dad,
who proudly continue
to buy photo albums

cont

introduction: where did awesome go?

TAKING PICTURES RUINS EVERYTHING.

Today life is captured with digital cameras, webcams, and mini camcorders, items that (literally) give us not only immediate gratification, but also the ability to hand-pick what makes us look best. And with the click-and-upload option readily available to anyone with a social networking account, we've all become the photo editors of our own personal tabloids. Gone is the candid portrait that illustrates genuine human emotion with faces and expressions that send our imaginations running. Instead we're left with an aesthetic that, in and of itself, *lacks* an aesthetic.

In fact, if there's any theme that carries through contemporary photos, it's narcissism. Narcissism fills every pore of MySpace, Facebook, and Twitter, leaving us with photos meticulously taken with specific intentions in mind (and immediately deleted if those objectives don't pan out). Some people even hire professional photographers to shoot the "perfect" profile photo, clearly illustrating that vanity has never run more rampant in our culture. Be it the "twee gaze" (usually taken in a sun-kissed field of reeds), or "aerial emo shot" (which is always shot from above, as if we're not supposed to realize that the subject is pushing his arm out of the frame for the most flattering angle), photos are seldom incidental now. They no longer just *happen*. We are all guilty of, essentially, trying to be something we're not: our photographed self.

Pictures of our parents and grandparents, however, tend to carry a clearer sense of happenstance, of a natural candidness that results less in coordinated (in)authenticity and more so in the capture of a real moment or era, a forgotten time and place. In other words, these photos represent that misplaced point in time when your parents were effortlessly *cool*.

That's why I started My Parents Were Awesome, a blog that collected vintage photos of readers' parents and grandparents. As someone with absolutely no background in photography, my intent for the site was merely to bring attention to something that was missing from the Internet: warmth. I realized that it was high time to supplement the endless barrage of shots featuring college pranks and half-naked ladies with a wholly different set of untapped resources: old photos and parental devotion.

When my dad, Larry, visited the University of Massachusetts at Amherst in 1976, he knew it was going to become his alma mater. Not long after settling in, he attended an on-campus Jewish shabbat service, where he met Leanne. Leanne was dating her future husband at the time, but she realized that this skinny, bearded boychick would make a great catch for her shy roommate, Sandi, whom Leanne had had to pry out of her dorm room that night.

While they now look back and laugh, remembering sitting Indian-style across from each other in a "hippie dippie" circle of undergrads that fall evening, their simple love story, a parable stripped of glamour and glitter, is what makes it so enchanting. While it's always pleasant to hear stories of star-crossed lovers reunited or spouses who met amid uncanny circumstances, the trusty "boy meets girl" standby can be equally captivating, and my parents' pedestrian way of finding each other is more than they need to understand their love.

Although my sister and I grew up on Long Island, Massachusetts was always the go-to destination for weekend vacations. My parents keep their meeting grounds close to their hearts, so, needless to say, I was likely one of *very few* kids to closely document trips to towns like Lee, North Adams, and Hadley in my travel journal as if I'd gone island-hopping in the Caribbean. Nevertheless, all the familiar sites my folks pointed out never quite made an impact on me until I truly understood how much significance they'd held: Rooster's, the greasy spoon where they ate breakfast for two dollars; the tobacco fields from which their dog, Sara, would return, covered in filth and reeking of manure; the restaurant where Dad played jazz gigs while Mom made more than twice as much cash waitressing. These places were the literal reminders of their time together before I showed up. And it was always so easy for me to take for granted the fact that there were, indeed, haunts and apartments and shitty jobs they called their own. It hadn't *always* been, as I'd lazily convinced myself, diapers and report cards and car pools and chicken nuggets and karate practice. My parents were once young adults who, in dating for three years before moving into a small house together where my mom was forced to turn her ring upside down as if she were wearing a wedding band (the landlord wouldn't have approved otherwise), simply enjoyed each other's company. They weren't hippies in the sense that they wore flowers in their hair and bum-rushed Crosby, Stills, & Nash concerts, per se, but they purposely sought out a quiet, cozy lifestyle far from their noisy New York roots, deep into New England countryside that they could cherish and share with their children for the rest of their lives—a decision that continues to make them nothing less than awesome.

And it's that sentiment that rings true in the photos from their youth, when developing film cost money and life wasn't one big fashion show. Larry and Sandi were just being themselves, and, luckily for me, someone was there to press the shutter.

—ELIOT GLAZER

my
parents
were
awesome

jimmy and paula

by Jamie Deen

I AM SO EXCITED TO HAVE the opportunity to contribute to this book, *My Parents Were Awesome,* because, well they *are* awesome. I got to digging around my old photo box looking for the perfect picture of my parents to submit and, lo and behold, two reasons why they are awesome jumped out of this photo that is more than forty years old.

First my mother, Paula Ann Hiers. Beauty queen. Cheerleader. The life of the party. I mean, her nickname was Poot. Poot as in fart. That's my momma. The personality she was born with is now enjoyed by millions of people, but in 1965 she only had eyes for my dad . . . Jimmy Deen. Bad boy. Wrong side of the tracks. Fast car. Marlboro Reds with a cold Bud racked up tight in the crotch cruising Slappey Boulevard on a Saturday night.

Which leads me to reason number one:

My mom doesn't judge people. Never ever. She took one look at Jimmy and was off. Riding shotgun in that fast car with her feet propped up on the dash, stealing a sip of cold beer while puffing on her own cigarette—menthol, of course. My mom didn't care where my dad came from, and loved him for the boy he was and the man that was sure to come.

Reason number two:

Look at that picture again. My dad was cool! Look at him. White dinner jacket with a thin little bow tie. Tan, rested, and ready. But look closer . . . down at his shoes . . . brown penny loafers. My dad didn't have the ability or finances to jaunt off to the shoe store and get a new pair of lace-ups for the big dance. What's a South Georgia boy to do? Make do, that's what. Shine up those Weejuns and cut a rug. The best part about the whole thing is he *owns* that outfit. After seeing this photo my wife said, "They were a really good-looking couple." You're damn right they were, as much for the brown shoes with a tux as anything else. Good luck solving the riddle of the papier-mâché face looming over my parents. I've asked for thirty-some odd years for an explanation and neither one has a clue what it meant.

In the year 1965 Jimmy proposed marriage to Paula and after a small wedding attended by family and friends, they lived happily ever after . . . until about 1971 anyway.

My mom lost both of her parents within a few years of each other. Grandfather Hiers passed away before I was born, and Grandmother Hiers went to Heaven right after my brother Bobby was born in 1970. Mom's brother, Bubba, was a teenager at the time and moved in with us. The loss of her parents coupled with the pressure of raising not only my brother and me, but her brother, too, proved to be too much. It was slow to come, but when I was in middle school my mom was a total agoraphobic.

My dad was raised in a family that had their own set of challenges. He came from a big family on a very small budget. The easiest way to classify his childhood was dysfunctional. People deal with situations differently, and at that time my dad self-medicated. Nothing illegal, mind you, but not within the boundaries my mom set . . . which were pretty damn tough considering her condition. Right now you may be thinking I'm taking a pretty strange route to the "My Parents Were Awesome" part, right?

Well, here's the awesome part:

My mom and dad loved us every day. More important, they told us every day and kissed us and hugged us. My dad kisses me on the mouth to this day and I'm a forty-two-year-old man. And you know what? I'm gonna kiss *my* son on the mouth until I'm pushing up dirt. A parent's love, y'all. That's awesome.

We also learned to let yesterday go. The past is in the past forever. Learn from your mistakes and try like hell not to repeat them. No regrets, y'all. That's awesome. We also learned from my parents the importance of not taking ourselves too seriously. When you laugh at yourself first, it drowns out the sound of everyone who is *really* laughing at you.

Love, a free spirit, and laughter. That's not a bad life plan. And the fact that we learned it from two kids born in South Georgia who were chewed up and tumbled through their early adulthoods is damn near a miracle.

The curtain came down on my parents' marriage after twenty-seven years but it proved to only be an intermission. My father has moved back to our hometown, Albany, Georgia, and married the woman he dated before he met my mom. He has straightened out all his curves in the road and taught me there is no way to measure the will of a man. I am as proud of him as I am of anything else in my life.

And my mom, well, you know about her already.

✻ ✻ ✻

Jamie Deen is one half of the Deen Brothers Incorporated and wants to be the best husband, father, son, and brother he can be.

eleanor and johnny

by Jennifer Mascia

I WAS ELEVEN WHEN I REALIZED my parents Did It.

It was sometime after science class in sixth grade, and I don't know how the conversation started, but before long, sitting on one of the steel benches outside our homeroom, Julian Garcia, Jessica Quimbo, and I had pieced together the origin of our existence: Somewhere, sometime, at least once, our mothers and fathers had given in to animal lust—the same animal lust we ourselves were on the threshold of feeling—and mashed their private parts together and Did It.

"Ewwww!" we screeched, writhing and restless, darting to and fro as if we could physically shake the utter grossness of this thought from our tender systems. But it was too late: The notion had been planted. Our parents had

had sex. And in Julian's and Jessica's cases, definitely more than once; I am an only child, but that was cold comfort in light of this icky revelation.

The thought of my parents having sex was horrific enough—unlike my classmates, my parents had birthed me in their forties, and imagining fifty-somethings doing the nasty was just too much for this prepubescent girl to handle—but from this idea, another evolved: My parents had lives before me. And that was downright barbaric.

My short life was all I knew, so certainly my life was all they knew, too. Right? But now I imagined that they must have had experiences that had nothing to do with me. Years full of them, in fact. It felt like cheating. They had cheated on me, with each other! How dare they!

Several years ago, not long after my father died (and a few years before my mother followed), I rescued my parents' phone-book-thick red and blue photo albums from the basement of my mother's apartment building, which flooded every winter like clockwork. Over her shrill objections—"Jenny, stop! They're full of mold!"—I carefully extracted hundreds of 1970s-era Polaroids from the soppy albums. Luckily, most of the snaps were untarnished, clear as if they'd been taken the day before, but some had been tinted blue from water damage, which actually gave them an artsy flair.

And there they were: Eleanor and Johnny in the Keys. Eleanor and Johnny mid-laugh, slightly stoned and loving it. Eleanor sitting on Johnny's lap, beaming with newly minted devotion, a cigarette dangling between her delicate fingers as his muscular, tattooed arms tightly encircled her waist. Johnny with his arm draped over Eleanor in the living room of his mother's house after she tasted her mother-in-law's marinara for the first time. (Years later my father would admit that my mother's red sauce was better, much to her delight.)

Forget about being a twinkle in their eye—I'm not even a fragment of a thought in these pictures. And though seeing them that young and carefree is undeniably a trip, that fact sends a shiver down my spine.

We can't help it—we think of ourselves as flesh-and-blood inevitabilities, wandering the earth, paying our taxes, emptying our DVRs, and it's chilling to think that there was a time when our existence wasn't so certain. An unexpected aberration—an untimely breakup, a "Honey, I have a headache," a condom that didn't break—and we wouldn't be here at all.

But there's also something charming about seeing our parents in their taut, sinewy prime. When those photos were taken, the petite, attractive brunette and her Italian roughneck boyfriend weren't Jenny's parents—they were Johnny Mascia and Eleanor Sacks of Brooklyn, New York. Those four eyes that stare back at me from 1975 haven't a clue as to what they would become, and without the weight of parental responsibility, they look so free. Weightless. Buoyant. And stylish! My mother's enviable waist, not yet thickened by childbirth, slithers into a smart white pantsuit. My father's hands, not yet swollen and calloused by years of carpet cleaning and installation, are gracefully splayed across my mother's demure shoulders. They don't know they are parents. They may as well be me and my boyfriend.

They also don't know they are dead. These Polaroids are all I have left of them, and for that I'm glad—no, *proud*—that I disobeyed my mother and rescued them from her dank Staten Island basement. My weakness for nostalgia came in handy after all.

And now, when I look at pictures of me and my boyfriend, I see that same childless innocence in our eyes. We glow in the embrace of fresh desire, and it dawns on me that someday soon my own waist will be thickened by childbirth, never to retract, and he will grow a rueful paunch, and in twenty years we'll look back at our own set of pictures and think, *We were awesome once, weren't we?*

And one day, these photos will be all our children have left of us.

✳ ✳ ✳

Jennifer Mascia received an MS from Columbia University's Graduate School of Journalism in 2007 and has spent the past four years as an editorial assistant on the Metro desk of *The New York Times.* Her memoir, *Never Tell Our Business to Strangers,* was published in 2010 by Villard.

steve and teena

by Mike Adamick

IT'S THE RED SHOES THAT GET me. I stare at this photo of
my parents—my dad poured into tight clothes, with his
belt pulled up around his naval; my mom in a blue-and-
white maternity dress dotted with red buttons that resem-
ble candy—and I wonder who these people are. Surely
they aren't related to me. Surely this isn't the same woman
who ruined my summer days of leisure, hauling me
around to thrift store after thrift store in search of "new"
shoes or purses or dresses.

The strangers in this ancient, sepia-tinged photo—
they're too put together. Too fashionable. Too, what's the
word? Cool.

It makes me cringe to even think it.

But I keep coming back to those shoes.

Flat and comfortable looking, they are the sensible kind of thing you'd probably wear if you're carrying around an extra ten pounds in your vagina. But at the same time, they gleam. They sparkle. They provide a perfect complement to the splay of red buttons running down my mom's elegant bodice, giving the appearance of a subdued Fourth of July party.

They match her outfit so perfectly that it makes me consider the idea that she had, at one time, thoughts revolving around things other than me—thoughts that centered on fashion and style and the kind of kicky little red shoes you might find on some innocent soul in an emerald world, her young heart bursting with song and promise. That's the thing that gets me. My mom was young once, and although this feels awkward to admit, this photo proves she was also good looking.

My mom had always told me that her first job was as a clerk at her local Montgomery Ward department store, and I had always filed away this information in some rarely dwelled-upon internal locker. She was young. She worked as a store clerk. Probably billions of American girls did the same thing. But now it occurs to me that she could have found a similar customer service job just about anywhere. She could have been a carhop or a burger flipper. She could have been the girl handing you slightly damp rented bowling shoes, smiling at the thought of making clowns for a living. But she chose a department store—a place filled with clothes. And I'm only now beginning to see why.

When I was a kid, my mom shopped at any and every thrift store she could find. Growing up, I never realized we might be hurting for money. It just felt normal to see her in some overly floral dress or toting around a leather purse with a frayed seam tucked snugly against her midsection, as if to hide it from view. Her shoes were always worn and creased, no matter that she had just purchased them the day before. She'd come home from a day of shopping, and in contrast with my friends' mothers—who littered their hallways with shopping bags and hatboxes—my mom returned with only the aroma of dust and attic.

"Oh they're just as good as any other clothes," she'd say, dumping her new . . . ish dresses in the washing machine for the first time in who knows how long.

I wouldn't necessarily use the word *frumpy* but it pained me to see my mom's horrible choice of clothes. I'd cluck my tongue and shake my head at her selections, sighing to myself and coming to terms with the idea that she just had no sense of fashion. No sense of style.

I grew up during the great Guess Jeans fad of the 1980s, yearning for the little green ass triangle to mark me as the apotheosis of cool. Add in Reebok Pumps and a leather bomber jacket from Aéropostale or one of those heat-sensitive shirts that changed color as you wore it, and I could have probably made a perfect stand-in for that kid on *Silver Spoons*. Oh how I wanted a train in my house.

I remember standing in the kitchen one afternoon, begging and pleading with my mom for a pair of Guess overalls—not so I could go around looking like a pint-sized farmer in the latest Italian denim, but so I could leave the straps dangling out from under my shirt like all my friends.

"Why not just buy jeans then?" my mom wondered. "They do the same thing and they're cheaper!"

Poor woman. Had she even heard of the word *cool*?

My mom looked down at her shoes for a moment. They were scuffed and the rubber on the heel tilted sharply to one side. She sighed and tossed a dishrag on the counter, agreeing that she could probably find a dress for her upcoming party "somewhere" although we both knew where that might be.

"Okay," she finally relented.

A few hours later, she took me to the mall, where she bought a pair of overalls from a clerk she knew—a clerk who gave her an employee discount and slid the jeans into a bag quickly, while looking around. My mom handed me the bag and patted my shoulder, smiling—probably off the look of joy in my eyes. Then we hit up Chik-fil-A for free samples and went to the Salvation Army to see what we might find for her.

I look at this photo now and see a different couple. From the bulge in my mom's belly and the time stamp on the back of the slim stock, I can guess she was pregnant with her middle child, my brother Jeff, whom we would lose seventeen years later. The family would break up after that. My dad, so young and full of energy in his formfitting yellow shirt, would become a drunk, seek help, and leave the family, taking what was left of a tiny nest egg and disappearing. If there were any photos from this era, we probably all would have looked broken and hopeless—the look of pain and quiet tragedies playing across our faces.

But in this older photo, my parents posing with smiles and arms slid unseen behind their backs, this distorted future seems impossible. This young, put-together couple looks too happy.

So it's the shoes that attract my attention now and make me see my mom in a different light all these years later. I wonder if, slipping them on that morning, clasping the buckles around her slim ankles, she had any inkling of the tragedies to come—the sacrifices she would make, the joys she would put off, all so her spoiled child could live in a world where things like fashion and being cool seemed so important. I wonder if she knew her future family would be living on borrowed time, waiting to break. I have a child of my own now and can finally appreciate all the sacrifices my mom made in the name of parenthood, because I realize now there isn't one thing I wouldn't give up in the name of my daughter's happiness. I look at these glistening, ruby-red shoes now and think of all the tattered shoes she exchanged them for in the years to come and all the things she silently went without, ceding a part of herself to a different song—a song still filled with promise. But for someone else entirely.

✳ ✳ ✳

Mike Adamick is a San Francisco stay-at-home dad whose writing regularly appears on National Public Radio and in the *San Francisco Chronicle*. When he's not teaching his four-year-old daughter to sew, he's usually curled up in the pretzel on the living-room carpet, regretting the time he taught her UFC arm bars and leg triangles.

tony and leeka

by Aaron Khefeits

MY DAD IS A NERD. He's a programmer, he works for Yahoo!, and his apartment is stacked floor-to-ceiling with math textbooks (80 percent of which he's read). He's a big science-fiction fan, but mostly Asimov, not Lucas. His wardrobe is strictly earth tones, usually made out of some kind of new microfiber blend that repels water, though he isn't clumsy or prone to spills.

He has that nerdy pragmatism that strips something down to its core function and reimagines a more efficient way to perform that function—which usually is also impossible or absurd. He believes that cooking should be left to professionals: It should be built into everyone's salary that they dine out for every meal. After all, if division of labor makes us more effective, why should one be any more expected to cook their own meals than to make their own shoes? He believes in real sex education: He once told me that he thought an experienced middle-aged prostitute (presupposition: Prostitution has already been legalized, regulated, and taxed) should come to a sex-ed class full of boys and really teach them what is going on. Not just the anatomy, safety measures, and the like, but also what they should be doing in the bedroom. No point in pussyfooting around.

It was because of this kind of pragmatism that I was a little surprised at some advice he gave me. I was with my girlfriend at her parents' North Carolina home, for what I had thought would be a wonderful week with the family I would soon join. It turned out to be a breakup visit. I lay on the floor sobbing heavily over what is still the most painful experience of my (admittedly sheltered) life. I called anyone whom I thought could help me get it together before she returned home that afternoon. Naturally, I thought of the person who could empathize, but also could tell me the practical move: my dad.

In uncharacteristically macho language, he gave me the following advice about the breakup: Don't. "You can't necessarily win this fight," he said, "but you can go down swinging." I was too focused on my own troubles to notice how out of character were both the content and the choice of words: My dad had never seen much value in any sort of fight, be it physical, emotional, or food. And it turned out that his advice wasn't all that practical, at least on the face of it. Rather than preventing a breakup, it protracted it over an excruciating and expensive six months during which I blew thousands of dollars on plane tickets, gifts, and phone cards, not to mention booze. Of course, none of these things helped the situation, except perhaps the booze.

When I had some perspective on this situation, I asked my dad where that advice had come from. I'd never asked about this before because I am a self-absorbed monster, but it turned out that he had a long history with women. Perhaps more accurately, my dad had a long history near women. At the age of thirteen, he'd had a sweetheart in Florida, but he moved with his family to California and by the time he brought himself to reconnect with her, she was married with a kid. He'd had a pretty serious girlfriend in his PhD program in statistics (I do not in any way exaggerate his nerdiness) but she called it off because "it wasn't going anywhere." His usual MO was to like a girl from a distance until finally he could work up the courage to like a different girl from a distance.

In a somewhat unnerdy way, he attended a New Year's Eve party (okay, it was a party for statistics graduate students, but unnerdy for him) and hit it off with a very cute recent transplant from the Soviet Union. With unnerdy bravado, he threw his cards on the table and asked her out. And was rejected. The next semester, he was the TA for her multivariate analysis class, so it wasn't hard to come up with excuses to ask her out a couple more times in the halls of the department. Rejected and rejected. He decided to try out something called "playing it cool" he had heard so much about. He played it cool for the entire semester, which basically meant no interaction between the two of them. He played it cool right up through the graduation party at which he met her husband. He even tried to play it cool after he stuck a toothpick halfway through his finger when he heard the word *husband* (again, for him that's pretty cool).

From there, the husband left them to chitchat. She mentioned wanting to visit some friends in Santa Cruz now that classes were out. My dad was standing there, toothpick literally in hand, reeling from the discovery that the cute Russian girl he had been teaching and flirting with for six months was married. That was a haymaker he had just walked right into. Reeling, most likely down for the count, he was able to say, "You know, my parents live right by there. It would be really cool if we could meet up. What's the number of your friend's place?" Dad has staggered to his feet. I don't know what the actual number was, but in my mind she just breaks into song with "Eight-six-seven-five-three-o-ni-he-ine." This round to Dad.

My dad called and got a dinner date in Santa Cruz. Why they couldn't have gotten dinner when they were both living within a mile of each other and sitting in class together every day is anyone's guess. They met for dinner at a romantic Italian place my dad knew and they got along well, as they always had. On the way out, my dad remarked, "You know, if we got struck by lightning right now, whoever found us might get the wrong idea." Is there a term in boxing for when someone knocks themselves out, falls on a nail, and gives themselves tetanus? A cooler person (read: anyone else) would know (a) not to say cheesy things; (b) not to say awkward things; and (c) not to say morbid things. A cooler person would not have gotten the response my dad did: "They might get the right idea." My dad then had a very cool thought: *I like this girl.*

They got married, had my brother, then me, and thereby ruined their lives. I think my dad gave me the advice he did because he wanted me to do the same. At the very least, he wanted me to never have to wonder if I could have saved that relationship. I would probably rather have a girlfriend, but still I am very grateful for that romantic, passionate unnerdy part of my dad. Probably because I owe that part my existence.

✳ ✳ ✳

Aaron Kheifets is a comedian, writer, and director. He is a contributing writer for the Onion News Network, and his writing and direction have been seen on Comedy Central. Like his dad, he is also a huge nerd.

bruno and elena

by Elia Bazan Garcia

HIS SKIN IS THE COLOR OF COFFEE, a long black with a touch of milk. His graying mustache and eyebrows are as thick as a hairy caterpillar. He slowly shuffles down the hallway wearing more than five layers of clothes. With every few steps, he pulls his pants up, as his body is too skinny to hold them on. Clasping a cigarette and a lighter in his left hand, he gives a cheeky look through his dirty glasses and smiles, revealing a million wrinkles of happiness. He sits down on a comfortable, throne-like chair and lights his cigarette, one of many for the day. He pulls the smoke in and looks to the ceiling. His eyes water as the smoke billows from his nose and mouth. The tears could be from the smoke but it seems more likely that he is feeling nostalgic.

"How to begin if I have lived three hundred years?" he contemplates, referring to the fact that he has experienced so much in seventy years.

Having a conversation with Bruno is as delightful as having a hot chocolate in front of a fireplace during a snowy evening. *Bruno* is the nickname he chose for himself, honoring an always wanted, but never conceived, third son.

His wife giggles to herself as she states, "Instead of Bruno you should call him Cabruno!" *Cabruno* is a word she made up combining *cabron* and *Bruno*. *Cabron* is Spanish for "asshole."

Bruno's parents were both Olympic basketball players and world athletes. He was born at the beginning of World War II in the streets of Mexico City where everybody knew one another and respected old traditions. Bruno spent most of his time as a little boy with his British grandma, Sarah Straffon, as his parents were always traveling.

"I loved my granny very much. She was always giving me candy and toys with the utmost tenderness and she made delicious desserts to pamper me," he reminisces.

Bruno was a very stubborn boy who rarely obeyed rules. He would do whatever he wanted, whenever he wanted. Every six months since he was born his parents took him and his older brother to a beach in Acapulco. When he was three years old, his dad rented a bus. He placed a cot in it so Bruno and his brother would be comfortable during the twelve-hour drive. They would arrive at the house of Dona Metri, who was married to Juan, a fisherman.

The place was nothing more than a *palapa,* a tiki hut with a roof of palm trees, walls made out of sticks, and hammocks.

One night when everybody was asleep, Bruno went outside to go to the toilet. Suddenly, something caught his attention. "I saw the ocean with lights, which were coming from the fishing boats. I went to the seashore to play as I always did. While I was playing, some fishermen saw me. They were worried that a three-year-old boy was on the beach by himself at night. They took me with them on their boats so I wouldn't be by myself. That was my first fishing experience."

When Bruno's parents noticed he was missing, they asked Dona Metri to call people in town for help. Soon most of the population of Acapulco, which was 350 at that time, was out looking for him. As the sun came up the community was praying against, but expecting to find his body in the water. Bruno's mum and dad were standing on the beach with the big crowd, feeling hopeless, not knowing what to do.

As the fishing boats returned with a big haul from a night at sea, Bruno's parents spotted a small figure at the front of one of them.

"The one who was standing at the front of the boat was me. I felt like Christopher Columbus on the *Santa Maria* as he discovered America. I was happily waving to my parents, eager to tell them about my awesome adventure, oblivious to what I had put them through." Unfortunately, his parents were not impressed by his display of independence. He was scolded and punished for disappearing in the middle of the night.

As Bruno told the story, he shared the thrill of the moment in such a way that any listener would have felt they had been in that boat with him. By this time he had already smoked his third cigarette. He came back to the present from his daydream and didn't speak another word. An expression of joy and pride was smeared across his face.

"Hold on, here's another one," he exclaimed, as he took a deep breath.

After the Acapulco holidays were over, Bruno's mum decided it was time for him to start school. It was the first day and the class was learning a dance. There were two circles of children, a circle of boys on the outside and a circle of girls on the inside. The boys were walking right and the girls were walking to the left. A girl walked past Bruno and poked her tongue out at him. This made him very angry. The next time she crossed, he pulled her dress up.

"At that time, girls were only allowed to wear skirts or dresses," he clarifies.

The teacher told him to stand outside the classroom as a consequence for his actions. While Bruno watched his classmates playing inside, the girl poked her tongue out at him again and he exploded in anger. He punched the window with his fist and smashed it. He didn't get hurt, but he was forced to stand by himself next to a fountain in the middle of the yard. Bruno was still upset and, adding to that, he felt bored and hot. He decided to take a swim but didn't want to share the water. He saw a net and one by one he caught all the fish in the fountain and threw them on the ground where they slowly died. He proceeded to take off his clothes. Now naked, he hopped into the water and began splashing it everywhere.

"Mum picked me up to the news that I was expelled from school after the first day of my educational life." Bruno chuckled cheekily.

With the sweetest of hearts, an outstanding intelligence, and amazing charisma, the seventy-year-old has a million anecdotes to share. These are only two from his first three years of life. He is so entertaining and captivating that five hours with him feel like three seconds; and a thousand pages wouldn't be enough to fit in his exciting and full life.

His wife of thirty-five years, Elena, describes being with Bruno as an unpredictable life full of highs and lows. She can be talking about the most serious topic with him and he unexpectedly interrupts her with the funniest of comments, which makes her burst into laughter.

"I've heard him say so many hilarious remarks, I often tell him I'm going to write a dictionary in alphabetical order of all the witty things he says. Besides, he has given me the biggest blessings of my life . . . my twin daughters. Bruno fainted when the doctor told us I was pregnant with two. They are now beautiful women inside and outside. I will always be grateful for that," Elena expresses emotionally.

After hearing his wife's comments, Bruno's eyes fill with tears again. He takes a deep breath and looks at the ceiling hoping to control his emotions.

"Everything I've done has been for God and in the name of God," he adds while lighting the fifth cigarette.

Emotions win the battle at this point. He stands up, leaving the partially extinguished cigarette smoldering in the ashtray, and walks away in silence to regain his composure. Five minutes later, he comes back smiling.

"Be happy is the name of the game," he affirms after giving a little skip. He takes his seat again and scratches his ears in excitement. He gives his characteristic high-pitched holler, which sounds similar to the call of a tropical bird, and exclaims, "Those stories were nothing. Here's a better one for you . . ."

✳ ✳ ✳

Elia Bazan Garcia is a Latin dance teacher. She was born and raised in Mexico City and currently lives on the Australian Gold Coast.

Her essay was chosen after being submitted in a contest on the website.

richard and jennifer

by Christian Lander

THESE ARE MY PARENTS ON THEIR wedding day in October 1967. It's one of the few photos my family still has from that era, but it's a great one.

They first met at Queens University in Kingston, Ontario, and anytime my father has had a glass of wine and wants to make me uncomfortable in a group setting he will tell the story of how they first started dating. He'll also be sure to lean into me in order to loudly announce he first noticed my mom because of "her tits." Needless to say that I made sure the first meeting with my future in-laws took place at a restaurant that didn't serve alcohol.

It didn't stop him.

Typically he will begin the story of his awareness of her breasts first occurring, as it does for so many others, in the university classroom. In his case it was a senior-year course in economics.

Though it might seem redundant at this point, it's important to know that my father is confident, brilliant, and a bit of a smart-ass. Okay, a lot of a smart-ass. And as we all know one of the hardwired traits of smart-asses is their inability to take any sort of schoolwork seriously. My father was no exception.

My mother, on the other hand, was absolutely neurotic about getting good grades. She stressed about every test, handed in assignments early, and worked extremely hard. Myself being both a smart-ass and a grade-grubbing neurotic, this part of the story, if nothing else, makes an understanding of genetics seem within my grasp.

During the course of the semester, while my mother was working, my father was scheming and searching for the right moment to make his move.

Unfortunately for my father, the semester came and went without any real progress. He was able to talk to her, get her name, and have a few short shallow conversations but ultimately nothing of any substance. When the final exam arrived, he knew that he had to make his move.

On the way into the exam, he wished her luck. She deflected his praise and simply tried to focus on the task at hand. This would be harder than he thought.

My father breezed through the test and spent the remaining time looking at my mother or thinking about Vietnam, or the USSR, or pranks, or whatever college students thought about in 1967. My mother spent every waking second writing in her exam book, and was doing so right up until the exam proctor attempted to pry it from her hands.

When the test let out, my father asked my mother about her performance.

"I failed," she said. "I know it."

"Oh bullshit," said my father. "I'm sure you did fine."

"No, I really think I failed this."

And there it was. My father's golden opportunity.

"I'll tell you what. I know for a fact you did better than me on this test."

"No," she said. "You're a good student, you're always talking in class."

"Uh sure," added my father. "But how about we make a deal? If you get a higher grade than me, then you have to sleep with me."

It goes without saying that this seems like a fairly ridiculous bet. What could my mother possibly get out of it? Other than the clap or whatever VD they cured with penicillin back in those days.

To be honest I'm not quite sure about my mother's logic in this situation. I assume she must have been confident that she had done poorly since she didn't even make my father agree to a contingency in the event that he got a higher grader than her. I suppose in that situation the only reward was that she didn't have to sleep with him.

Unsurprisingly, my hardworking mother did end up getting a higher grade than my father. And, proving his worth as a husband, my father did not force her to honor the bet.

Although when you think about it my very existence proves that he collected on his bet . . . that one time in 1978 nine months before I was born . . . then again in 1979 before my brother was born. And that was it.

But this photo only begins to tell the story of my parents and their wedding day.

My father came from the Canadian equivalent of *Leave It to Beaver*. My grandfather owned a hardware store and my grandmother was a homemaker. They lived in a beautiful, love-filled house in small-town Ontario. My dad has stories about 45s, sock hops, poodle skirts, station wagons, and everything else you would expect from a child of the baby boom.

My mother, on the other hand, was born in England immediately after the war to two strict English parents who considered lettuce to be an ethnic food. When my mother was fourteen, they left England behind and moved to Canada.

My mother had hoped that her life would be new in all capacities; she was wrong. Her parents continued to show outlandish favoritism to her older brother, and the food continued to be boiled meat and potatoes. To make matters worse she was teased at school for her British accent and actually worked hard to lose it so she would fit in with the other Canadian children.

Her high school years were essentially one giant countdown until the day that she could leave for university and never come home. Unfortunately, fully breaking away from our parents and their expectations is always easier said than done.

At about the time that this photo was taken, my mother had been considering applying to medical school to become a doctor. She had the grades, she had the brains, and she had the drive. But her mother forbade her from applying because "women aren't supposed to be doctors." It's easy to say in retrospect that she should have told her parents to piss off and just gone anyway. But it was 1967 and it's impossible to fully understand what she was going through.

Thankfully, this picture doesn't conjure up any of that sadness or disappointment. Instead when I look at this picture, I see the first day that my mom finally could live the life that she always wanted and the life that she would ultimately give to me, my brother, and of course my father.

But as much as I love looking at this photo, there are times when I actually detest looking at it. Sure, I love to see it for the heart-warming story of my mom leaving her parents, and I love how beautiful my mother looks with her hipster mod haircut.

What I hate is looking at my father.

I don't hate it because I have pent-up resentment about my father collecting on that bet in 1978. I don't hate it because I have an Oedipus complex. No, what bugs me most is the simple fact that my dad looks fantastic. The glasses, the skinny tie, the haircut. He looks like he's about to leave tomorrow to write an *Esquire* feature on William Burroughs.

If there were to be some ripple in the space–time continuum that allowed my current self to go out to bars with the version of my father in this photo he would be universally recognized as better dressed and cooler than me. For a son, this can almost be too much to bear. Okay, now that I think about it, maybe I do have some sort of fashion Oedipus complex.

But the thing about the picture that really bugs me is that skinny black tie.

You see, when I was married in 2007 I also wore a black suit with a skinny tie. We have tons of photos of me in this outfit, and in none of them do I look better than my father. He was in better shape, his suit had a better cut, and his style was just generally superior to me in every possible way.

To me, this photo is the embodiment of what marriage should be: two people starting a new life together, one that will be better together than it was alone. I guess this photo also sums up the collective dreams of fathers throughout time: to be better looking than your son and have evidence that, yes, you were awesome.

Born and raised in Toronto, Christian Lander developed his sense of humor from his father and his neuroses from his mother. He is the author of *Stuff White People Like* and lives in Los Angeles with his wife, Jessica.

bob and kitty

by Mindy Raf

I'M IN MICHIGAN COMBING THROUGH THE contents of a rarely opened dresser drawer full of gems that haven't seen the light of day in decades. There's a shiny blue unitard from 1985, seamed pantyhose from 1955, and lots of lingerie from 1975 that simultaneously fills me with pride and nausea. I'm looking for a bathing suit because my sister and I just decided to head to a friend's pool. We don't want to look pasty in our off-white bridesmaid dresses at my brother's wedding tomorrow. (We end up looking red instead, with tacky tan lines to boot—but that's another picture for another book.)

I'm expecting to find a bunch of "momsuits"* in the

*momsuit \mäm sut\ n. 1. a garment worn for swimming that a daughter wouldn't be caught dead in. 2. a one-piece swimsuit with a skirt attached drawer, so I'm ecstatic when I spot a bikini top peeking out from underneath some holey leg warmers. I find the matching bottom, try it on, and head to the kitchen to model my find.

"Where did this come from?" I ask.

My mom glances up at me, says, "Oh, I lost my virginity in that suit," and then continues chopping up her cucumber.

I manage to swallow down the tablespoon of fresh throw-up in my mouth to say, "What?"

"No, just kidding," she says, popping a baby carrot into her mouth. "Well, maybe I did. I think that was from our honeymoon. What a nafka suit!"

Nafka, in our household, is Yiddish for "prostitute." Though it's hard to believe my mom wore anything remotely resembling a nafka as she cuts up vegetables in her tapered jeans and Liz Claiborne sweater set.

"Your boobs are gonna fry like bacon in that," she adds.

We're leaving for the airport in half an hour, so I have to move fast if I want to get all these boxes up to my bedroom, the safe zone. My dad is on a rampage. He's cleaning out the basement, and nothing is safe from the giant dumpster sitting in our driveway.

"Dad, these are pictures, albums, letters, you can't just throw all this out!"

"Whatever you want to keep, put in your room—anything left is getting tossed."

I want to respond with something like *Ugh, what is wrong with you?* but I don't because I'm afraid I'll start crying, and I don't want

to it, and/or lots of "business" going on in the midsection, e.g., pleats, ruffles, layers of mesh, and/or an attached belt of matching fabric with a rhinestone buckle. —momsuit-like, *adj.*

to get snot and salt water on any of the loose photos. So instead I respond with, "Okay, let's take them up to my room."

I have ten minutes until we leave and I'm desperately flipping through all the old albums, shimmying out pictures, and sticking them in ziplock bags. Maybe the more pictures I can take back with me to Brooklyn, the less I'll miss my mom. Then I find this one of my parents at the pool. My mom in that bikini that may or may not have been ripped off her body in newlywed passion soon after it was taken. I extract the picture from its plastic case and carefully seal it in a bag. I think I'll hang it on my wall when I get home. And then when people ask, "Oh, are those your parents?" I can say, "Yup, that was taken right before my mom maybe lost her virginity." And then they'll say, "Oh . . . okay . . ." I think she'd approve.

A little over the two-year mark is when the inquiries about fixing my dad up begin. Soon, every conversation I have with a Jewish person who lives in or has a connection to the state of Michigan starts out with, "Oh! Do I have a woman for your father . . ."

One night over the phone, I'm telling him about the latest inquiry—a high school friend who wants to fix him up with her mother's friend's cousin's sister's co-worker.

"Well, do you even want to . . . date?" I ask hesitantly.

"Well, the thing is, Mindy . . . your mother, you know . . . she was a knockout" is all he says. And I'm not sure if it's the way he says "knockout" or the sound of his sigh that follows, but I know he means it in a way that goes beyond finding her overwhelmingly attractive, beyond her mid-twenties bikini bod.

My dad and I talk more that night than we usually do. We trade memories, and share some funny *what would Kitty do if she were here* moments. It's the first time I remember us breaking out of our familial roles and just talking, the way my mom and I had started to do. I mention some of the old pictures I took, and how I now have them on my wall.

"Oh . . . that's nice. So you have them hanging up there, in Brooklyn?"

"Yup."

"That's nice."

"I can bring some back—or I was thinking of scanning them, so I can just email them all to you if you want."

"No, no, don't go to all the trouble. I've got the memories."

I've always loved that about my dad. Yes I was frustrated when I saw those dumpsters in our driveway, but I've always found his logic, especially lately, extremely comforting. It makes perfect sense, too, being satisfied with your memories. Still, I love having old pictures of my mom hanging on my wall to remind me that she existed long before she was my mom, or published in a book to show me, and all of you, that my parents were indeed awesome.

"But I'm glad we have those pictures," he adds.

Me too.

Mindy Raf is a writer, comedienne, and musician out of Brooklyn, New York. She's been a featured "talking head" on VH1's *Best Night Ever,* a comedy writer and voice-over artist for WABC radio, and the author of a widely read relationship column on CollegeHumor.com that has been featured in *The New Yorker* and the *New York Post.* She is currently finishing up her first novel, which is set to be published by Dial Books for Young Readers, a division of Penguin.

elaine and jerry

by Mike Sacks

MY PARENTS WERE NEVER REALLY COOL, and I think that's a blessing. If given the choice, I'd have greatly preferred to have parents who didn't wear kick-ass clothing bought at the hippest store in the most happening of indoor malls. Or who longed to wear the funkiest jewelry advertised in the most recent issue of *Cosmo*. Or whose biggest dream was to drive the same style of souped-up sports car Tubbs tooled around in on *Miami Vice*. I imagine it would have been a bit sad, even to a preteen geek like myself.

Then again, what *would* it have been like to have hip parents? The type who mysteriously jetted off on a solo vacation, sans kids, twice a year? Smoked dope? Danced through the house to the music played on Q107? Weren't such sticklers for homework and such?

The photo you see here was taken in San Juan, Puerto Rico, in 1979. My parents were just about to hit the hotel's club. This was new territory for them, two creatures in disco camouflage, totally out of their element. Two gentle critters about to lurk into a strange, potentially dangerous habitat that they'd heard about but never actually witnessed for themselves. It was time to make that leap.

And they did.

The resulting story emerged, with much excitement, from our eighteen-year-old cousin who was in the disco that night, and everything was recounted, in great detail, the next morning over virgin piña coladas at the hotel's swim-up bar. It went something like this:

My parents enter the bar in a manner resembling the kids who stumble into Wonka's chocolate factory: cautiously and awkwardly, but wide-eyed at the splendor of it all.

Standing within ten feet of the door, my parents wait out the first verse of the song. And the second. A table is found by the third or so verse.

My parents motion to an attractive waitress (who is wearing a very short skirt) and an order is placed. Drinks ordered all around. And food. It looks like wine and something fried. My cousin isn't sure. My parents rise during "Ring My Bell" and make their way to the dance floor. "Ring My Bell" ends, and "A Fifth of Beethoven" begins.

My parents appear to hold their own among the more regular set of dancers. My father kisses my mother on the cheek and my mother laughs. My father kisses my mother again and, again, she laughs.

At this point, all communication is lost. My cousin heads out to hit up another dance club. My parents aren't seen for the rest of the night. Presumably they had a wonderful time and only left a few minutes before the bar closed, along with everyone else.

This is where I picked up the thread.

Back in the hotel room, my younger brother and I had spent the hour or so since my parents left for the evening watching television and reading comics. And trying to imagine what could possibly be taking place in La Concha, the hotel's bar, a few stories below us. Disco dancing on tables. Whipping and cavorting bodies in syncopated beat to the hot, urban music. My father, drunk off an adult-type drink, scooting across the pulsating floor, much like John Travolta in that adult movie, but doing it more flamboyantly. Perhaps with a cape. Or a sparkly cane.

Man, it just had to be fantastic. They would be home after midnight, no doubt, perhaps escorted by hotel security, or being trailed by a local Puerto Rican TV news crew—

Actually, here they are now. And what's this? It's only about eight thirty, and they're not looking so hot. Both are complaining about the cigarette smoke, which is stinking up their clothes and making them both "nauseated." Both are temporarily deaf, due to the "horribly loud music" blasting "inches" from their table. Both are suffering "ferocious" headaches, not from alcoholic drinks (both were drinking "club soda"), but from the "commotion" and the "hubbub." Both were "ready to be back."

Truthfully, as exciting as we imagined their night to have been (or hoped to have been), my brother and I were ready to have our parents back. It was always fun to be together, and it still wasn't too late to hit the small restaurant across the street for some *jugo de china* (orange juice) and muffins (preferably blueberry). And then maybe a short walk along the beach. And then maybe a little TV, before bed.

I'm happy that my parents' cool quotient never reached beyond this photo, which may very well capture them at the pinnacle of their hipness. That's not to say that you can't be a good parent if you party often, or read through every issue of *Cosmo,* or skirt around town in a heavily modified Corvette, but as entertaining as the stories would be now for my adult self, I have a feeling that my brother and I wouldn't have been so amused at the time. Thank you, Mom and Dad! From thirty years on, you still look fabulous . . .

✳ ✳ ✳

Mike Sacks has written for *Vanity Fair, The New Yorker, Esquire, GQ, Time, Vice, McSweeney's, Believer, Radar, Salon,* and other publications. His book *And Here's the Kicker: Conversations with 21 Top Humor Writers* was published by Writer's Digest Books in July 2009. His second book, *Sex: Our Bodies, Our Junk,* was released by Random House in August 2010. And his third book, *This Begets That,* will be released by Tin House Books in spring 2011.

josephine and jim

by Salena Landon Reese

A FEW YEARS AGO, MY GRANDMOTHER slipped on the wood floors while wearing the totally unsafe tractionless knit booties with little balls on the heels that she stubbornly insisted on sporting well into her eighties. The fall landed her in the hospital, where my sisters and I took turns staying with her while her hip rehabilitated. During our visits, she talked for hours, literally, stopping only occasionally to sip on some cranberry juice to rewet her mouth. One afternoon, while drifting into a Percocet-induced sleep, she mumbled quietly, "I have so many things to say. I have so many stories. My mind is still nineteen . . . I'm just so old on the outside."

Now that she's truly gone away, and I can't shush her and tell her I've heard enough for now and count on her to tell me more next time I visit, I wish I had put her life on paper, all her stories in one place. In short, they are the stories of an old Italian woman who was once a vibrant, beautiful, redheaded girl who just happened to wake up one morning to find that nearly eighty years had passed. This is one of those stories.

In the spring of 1945, World War II was just a few short months from ending, but my grandmother Josephine didn't know that. What she did know, as she readied for her date on a sunny Saturday afternoon, was that she was eighteen, in love with a sailor, Jim, who was to be deployed in ten days, and couldn't wait for the evening ahead of her. Jim picked her up promptly, and they drove to Garrett Mountain, a sprawling, forested park in Paterson, New Jersey, and in those days a favorite place to find yourself alone with your significant other.

"He was off to war in ten days," my grandmother would exclaim while telling us, defensive, as though her decision were on trial. "You can imagine why we wanted to be alone!"

Unfortunately, Jim's adventurous nature wasn't limited to the seas, and rather than settling comfortably on a bench with Josephine, he insisted on exploring the property. After a short walk, they found themselves at the heavy iron gates of Lambert Castle, an enormous stone castle built in the 1890s by a British immigrant who wanted his own piece of royalty in the rural New Jersey area. At the start of the war, the castle had been closed to the public and used as an observatory to watch for enemy planes.

On this day, however, the black gates were open, the chain and padlock hanging unclasped. My grandfather, eyeing the large military equipment scattered about, suggested they enter the castle. Never one to be outdone by a man, Josephine charged forward, pointing to the highest tower, and they climbed to the top, noting the dusty, abandoned rooms as they ascended. They tried several doors, but all were rusting, locked, out of use for decades. They finally found an opening on the second floor leading into the tower. The small window overlooked the whole city—beautiful and serene as the sun set. They took in the sights, talking about their families, his leave, their future life together.

"Then," my grandmother would say, "he moved right in to kiss me. He was a sailor—they weren't the most trustworthy men in the world!" She would purse her lips, condemning the action, as though she was simply an innocent bystander, though our raised eyebrows always brought on a guilty smile.

After a short time, their attention was caught by the metallic sound of gates clanking together. They looked at each other in alarm, and Jim ran down the stone steps in a panic, nervous that they had been caught in an off-limits area of the park. What he found, however, was that the heavy entrance doors had been shut and bolted from the outside. He raced back up the steps, into the tower room, and to the barred window, but the guard had already descended the mountain, and Jim's calls for help were unheard.

For the next hour, Jim worked on budging the window bars, scraping their cement bases, bit by bit, a little farther apart. When they had finally budged, leaving a larger gap, my grandmother took off her shoes and readied to climb out.

"I was much smaller than him," she would tell us. "It only made sense. But no, he wouldn't have it. Stubborn." She'd point her finger at us, telling us to take notes and avoid stubborn men at all costs.

Instead, Jim, a strong, broad-shouldered man, wedged himself carefully through the bars, getting stuck quite a few times before finally dropping fifteen feet to the patio below. He promised to return with rope, and turned, running down the mountain toward the parking lot nearly a mile away.

"At that point," my grandmother would say, shaking her head, "I wasn't overly confident that he would come back for me! Like I said . . . sailors."

Nearly half an hour later, puffing and sweaty, and in the near dark, Jim returned carrying a length of rope from the trunk of his car. He tossed it up through the window, and my grandmother, a former Girl Scout, went to work knotting it around the bars. She dropped her shoes out the window first, and then eased out, holding the rope, and proceeded to slide down.

"It wasn't ideal," she would tell me, her eyes wide, thin arched brows raised. "In those days, we just didn't wear slacks, and there I was, sliding down onto the shoulders of my boyfriend." She always gave a single nod of her head, as though affirming just how scandalous the situation truly was for her.

Landing safely on the ground, the two took off running, leaving the rope dangling from the tower window and laughing hysterically at the circumstances. As they neared the car, Jim stopped her, spun her to face him, and took her hand.

"I wanted to do this earlier, but, like always with you, ginger-snaps, nothing is easy," he said, getting down on one knee in the gravel.

He pulled out a small gold band with a single diamond set on top and asked her to marry him.

"Well," my grandmother would tell us, shrugging and rolling her eyes as though it were just a silly question she decided to answer. "Of course, I said yes. After that day, who wouldn't?"

My grandparents married the next year, and though they divorced forty-five years later, my grandmother still smiles when she tells the story of how her life with him began.

✳ ✳ ✳

Salena Landon Reese lives in the Poconos with her husband, Ryan, and their lovable Great Dane, Kacie. She teaches writing full-time at a college in New Jersey. Her short stories have been published in *Calliope* and selected for publication in the *Best of the 2006 Penknife Press Short Story Writing Contest Entries*. She is a graduate of the Creative Writing MA Program at Wilkes University, and she is currently completing her first novel.

Her essay was chosen after being submitted in a contest on the website.

lil and jon

by Sara Benincasa

FOR ME, THE MOST SURPRISING THING about becoming an adult was discovering that I actually liked my dad. It definitely hadn't always been that way. At times throughout my childhood I'm fairly certain we mutually despised each other, though he might protest that he never, ever stopped loving me. As if you can't love someone and hate them in equal measure at the same time. For most of my upbringing, I'd say he thought I was brilliant and selfish and I thought he was brilliant and, well, selfish. We fought a lot.

In a way, I think we grew up together. Young parents and their kids often do. I was born when he was twenty-four. I'm aware it's not a young age for a father from a biological perspective. But having reached and passed the age of twenty-four a few years back, I can say with some certainty that the average twenty-four-year-old American adult male is not prepared for fatherhood—not in our culture of perpetual youth, of forever-adolescence. I know things were different in 1980, when I was born, and that my father did not emerge from the type of fast-paced, cosmopolitan lifestyle in which delayed adulthood was (and remains) the norm. Having a daughter at twenty-four probably made more sense to him than doing key bumps with Elton John somewhere in Manhattan, which I assume is what his hip, cool big-city contemporaries were up to. (For some reason, everything I envision about the 1970s and early 1980s involves Sir Elton John and cocaine.)

Last weekend, my younger brother came over to my rented studio apartment to help me build an IKEA wardrobe—by which I mean he built it and I helped a little, mostly by keeping him in a steady supply of Guinness. He saw a picture of my father and mother holding me on my first Easter, and noted that Dad looked kind of scared. I studied it later, and I don't quite agree. Overwhelmed, perhaps; a bit of a deer-caught-in-the-headlights type of look. But not scared, exactly. (Mom, on the other hand, looks peaceful and sleepy.)

It is strange to realize that my existence was more or less a planned affair. When I hear of twenty-four-year-olds getting pregnant today, I assume someone forgot to take her Pill, or put on his condom, or both. But actually, my parents had been married since my father was twenty-two and my mother was twenty-one, and they worked various low-paying jobs and still managed to own—*own!*—a house. I was as much a part of their plan as the three-bedroom ranch-style dwelling with the pear trees and the forsythia bushes in the back-yard. Dad had a white-dude 'fro of curly red hair, and was probably a full six feet back then. He always had pale skin and freckles and burned easily in the sun. Mom was tiny, about five foot one, and had luminous olive skin and lovely black hair that betrayed her Italian background. Somehow, this overgrown leprechaun and pint-sized Mediterranean mermaid brought forth a son and daughter who look like the nice Jewish girl and boy your parents always wanted you to marry. Be warned: We are nice, but we are not of your tribe.

My father spent a lot of his thirties and forties in a state of high stress, for a variety of reasons. As it happened, I also spent a lot of his thirties and forties in a state of high stress, some of which I chalk up to adolescence, some of which I chalk up to an emerging pattern of mental illness. We clashed often.

I have a hazy memory of actually trying to punch him in the face when I was a teen, a quixotic endeavor at best. This is actually a traditional Irish rite of passage, though it's generally the son who tries to knock his father out, usually at a drunken family wake in which the words "It was you that killed Ma! With yer drinkin', and your lyin'!" or "Little Brigid would still be here if not fer you!" are uttered at a high volume. In this case, I was just really incensed, probably the angriest I've ever been, and no one was drunk or dead or named Brigid. I'm not sure if he remembers it. I can say I did not have the pugilistic success of one of his personal heroes, Muhammad Ali.

Raising a child with a sometimes debilitating mental illness cannot possibly be a simple task, no matter the extent of your previous experience with the ailment in question (either as a sufferer or as a caregiver). My mother bore the brunt of dealing with my periodic and ever-worsening descents into panic and depression. However, my father also contributed time and time again to my road back to health, as much by what he didn't say as by what he did.

He did not, for example, call me crazy, or weak, or accuse me of pretending when I haltingly explained some of the things I felt. Parents are generally smart enough to realize that they never get the entire story, and if a kid says she's thought about killing herself once or twice, you can generally multiply that by fifty to one hundred. He just listened, and nodded, and patted me on the back, and took me to the doctor. On the way, he said it was all going to be okay, I'd see, just wait.

Once, when I was a baby, my dad sat in a rocking chair with me and held me until I fell asleep. He has a great affinity for babies, and they bring him joy and peace—which in turn tends to make him sleepy. That particular day, my twenty-four-year-old, overworked, underpaid, semi-clueless, probably-totally-freaked-out dad relaxed so much that he fell into a slumber of his own. His arms relaxed, and I rolled down his torso and legs into the crook of his feet. I didn't scream or cry. I didn't even wake up. We were just there, breathing together, two bundles of nerves and feelings, sleeping in tandem, and even asleep we both knew we were safe.

Shortly thereafter, my mother appeared and raised holy hell, as was her right. Having carried me successfully inside her body for nine months, she was naturally peeved that my father could not carry me for ten minutes without falling asleep on the job. Dad protested that it was my mother's yelling that caused me to wake up and start screaming. In a sense, he was right; I have always been painfully sensitive to my mother's shifts in moods, a tendency that I later learned to curb by holding her at a distance, sometimes harshly. My dad laughs about the story now, and teases my mom. I have to say that if my future baby daddy ever falls asleep while sitting up-right and holding my spawn, my reaction will mostly likely not be sunshine and cupcakes, either.

But the key element I take away from the story is this: Even when he screwed up and fell asleep on the job, he didn't drop me. He still held me up, by the skin of his teeth or the crook of his feet. His heart—and his ankles—were in the right place, even if his brain was on vacation. And so as an adult, I've come to define what I want in a partner not by whether or not he drops the ball, but by whether he manages, somehow, to catch it at the last second. And to try harder next time. And to forgive himself for fucking up. And to laugh about it later.

No matter how hard I tried, he never let me hit the ground. And I think that's pretty fucking awesome.

Sara Benincasa uses her mother's maiden name, but it's not because she doesn't think her dad rules. She was born a Donnelly in New Jersey, and now she hosts a sex talk show on Sirius XM. She's appeared on NBC, CNN, MTV, CBS, and a comedy stage near you.

seymour

by David Kamp

WAS THERE EVER A BETTER AUTOMOTIVE sales team than the classic DeAngelis Buick lineup of the '60s and '70s, that veritable Murderers' Row of the Central Jersey motor trade? You had Jack Moskowitz, Dick Summers, and Rene Abril on the showroom floor, and, holding down the sales manager's office, Seymour Kamp. The same four guys for twenty years, almost—you just don't see that kind of dynastic continuity anymore. I had the pleasure of watching this team in action, and let me tell you, there was never a quartet more charismatic and scrupulous in its pursuit of making its customers' V8-engine fantasies come true.

DeAngelis had a magnificent art deco showroom—the skinny tip of a long, trapezoidal building that occupied its own triangular island between French Street and Jersey Avenue in downtown New Brunswick—and these men, in their John Weitz suits and ASK ME ABOUT BUICK VALUE lapel pins, worked it with appropriate dignity, strolling up to customers casually, never in a caffeinated hustle. Kamp, especially, was extraordinary: a magnetic force with his booming voice and football player's build. (He played tackle on both offense and defense for New Brunswick High in the '40s.) People bought six, seven, eight cars from him and sent their friends to do the same—"Whatever you need, see Seymour!" the newspaper ads said. Those who didn't recognize his face from the paper knew his voice from the radio commercials he did on WCTC-AM, in which he pluggerooed the latest Electras, LeSabres, and Regals in a rat-a-tat delivery so rapid that the copywriters had to give him twenty-six lines of text to fill a minute of airtime rather than the requisite twenty-four. Even today, Jack Ellery, the radio host who manned the drive-time shift on CTC in that era and intro'd the ads with an offhand "Now let's hear from Seymour Kamp—Mr. Buick," ranks Kamp as one of Central Jersey's top three all-time merchant celebrities of the airwaves, along with the clothiers Wally Steinberg of Steinberg's Men's Shop and Norman Miller of Miller's on the Mall.

I reveled in being the son of Mr. Buick. (Prince Buick?) It wasn't even so much that his customers admired his honesty (though he *was* honest, and cringed at TV portrayals of loud-jacketed, sleazy car salesmen) as they valued his friendship and company. They brought him things—steaks, Knicks tickets, bottles of scotch he never drank—and he kept in touch after the sale, making house calls when their cars wouldn't start, dropping everything to hurry over with the jumper cables he always kept in his trunk. The man was verily invested in his burg, being a member of two synagogues, the junior chamber of commerce (president, 1956–57), the Rotary Club (chairman, program committee), the Elks (Lodge #324), and the Masons (Lodge #240), and he knew his Buicks inside and out, studiously attending the training sessions up in Union where men from Detroit explained the latest about wheelbases and gas-tank capacity. These twin faiths—to community and brand—conspired to make Mr. Buick the consummate local salesman, a trusted neighborhood vendor like your greengrocer, butcher, or dry cleaner, except his goods weighed two tons apiece and arrived on a trailer from Flint, Michigan.

The showroom was mine to roam whenever I visited, its boattail Riviera coupes mine to climb into and pretend-drive. (I liked the Rivieras best because they came with whitewall tires and had the highest sticker price.) I loved the aspirational gleam of the place, though I wouldn't have called it that then—the way its crenellated outer walls made it look like a castle and the way its sparkly, speed-lined, sunny interior, with exposures to the north, east, and west, suggested an open vista of happy motoring. Having a car-salesman father, furthermore, did wonders for my standing in school. For one thing, the other kids found my father's job more tangible and fundamentally uplifting than their fathers'—exactly what does an arbitrator or a professor of mechanical engineering *do*? For another, my father was, well, *Mr. Buick,* with all that it entailed. They heard him on the radio as they ate their breakfast in the morning, tagged along as their parents bought cars from him, wrapped their textbooks in the protective book covers he supplied to the schools (featuring prints of antique-model Buicks, naturally), and envied us Kamps for the fact that we got a new car every single year, even if it was a dealer demo that technically wasn't ours.

At home, we lived a life of intense Buick loyalty. We knew that the Buick wasn't tip-top of the line, that General Motors considered Cadillac its marquee luxury brand, and that the very word *Buick* was absurd, a reliable laugh-getter for comedians. But Buicks suited us, their quiet respectability simpatico with our unpretentious way of life. Our basement was festooned by my sister, brother, and me with surplus paraphernalia from the dealership, its support pillars adorned with DeAngelis bumper stickers and labels that said BUILT WITH GENUINE GM PARTS, its walls papered with circular posters bearing the words THE NUMBER ONE LITTLE ONE, leftovers from a promotion for the Opel, the crapola German-manufactured compact that gave Buick a foothold in the small-car market.

Seemingly half of our worldly possessions were the booty of sales contests put on by the Buick Motor Division, redemptions of the gift points my father accrued for every car he sold—our beds, our camping equipment, our clocks, our record player, our Lenox china, the little cordial glasses with the words BUICK SALESMASTER etched into them (which we used as ceremonial wineglasses during Passover seders), and the huge, chunky gold rings with tigereye insets, each more elaborate than the next, that my father received every time he surpassed another sales milestone. And also the binoculars in the dimpled-leather case autographed by Muhammad Ali. My father spotted a Rolls-Royce convertible on the shoulder of the New Jersey Turnpike one day in 1971, pulled over, and saw who the driver was. "Car trouble, Champ?" he asked. "Naw," said Ali, "it's just gettin' cold! I'm puttin' the roof up." Dad had a ballpoint, but neither he nor Ali had a piece of paper. The binoculars case had to do.

Your friendly DeAngelis sales staff: Jack Moskowitz, lean and affable, looked to me like Gene Rayburn; Dick Summers, white-haired and a little aloof, was Johnny Carson; and Rene Abril, diminutive, suave, and ethnic (Cuban, actually) . . . well, maybe he was Fred De Cordova. That I saw them in these roles, of unreconstructed mid-century men hanging on in the jive-turkey 1970s, is revealing, for I realize now that the world I was witnessing was already an anachronism, a spectral glimpse of what America used to be—not unlike the Doc Severinsen–conducted swing band that Carson stubbornly kept on his show even as the whole world around him went druggy and electric. The DeAngelis showroom was redolent of cologne, hair tonic, and cigarette smoke, a man's province; the "girls" who answered the phones did so from segregated balcony offices that overlooked the sales floor. It was all so irretrievably *adult,* with no heed paid to the fun-fun-fun teenybop car culture that was migrating eastward from California, no acknowledgment of an impatient, capricious "youth market" that needed to be flattered and dazzled with sweet rides and kustom-kool stereos. A swinging door behind Dick Summers's cubicle led back to an even more time-warped world: the cavernously dark body shop, which was populated with gnarled mechanics straight out of Walker Evans photographs, some of whom had been with the dealership since it was DeAngelis Nash in the 1930s. These apparitional figures kept up the illusion—within the walls of the strange, sarcophagus-shaped building, anyway—that New Brunswick remained a vital industrial city.

But half a mile from DeAngelis Buick, in the heart of the city's commercial district, the urban rot had set in. Albany Street, the main drag of my father's boyhood, had become a blaxploitation thoroughfare of head shops, empty storefronts, and glorious old deco cinemas reduced to showing porn; you half expected everyone to be walking in slanted, freaky gaits like R. Crumb characters. The original Tops Appliance store had been on Albany, its proprietor another local merchant-celebrity, Les Turchin, the man whose ubiquitous newspaper ads depicted him as "Topsy," a pointy-hatted cartoon figure with Hebraic features so grotesquely rendered that he looked like some hateful caricature out of *Der Stürmer.* But Les, ambitious and savvy, could see that Albany Street was going down the tubes; he moved his whole operation to a strip mall in Edison, where his giant new store, renamed Tops Appliance City, begat further mall megastores that siphoned business from New Jersey's dying downtowns. This circumstance so panicked the city's administrators and Johnson & Johnson, its major corporate presence, that they would eventually level the whole strip and replace it with an antiseptic complex of office buildings and esplanade shops, a faithful re-creation of some lame-ass urban planner's diorama.

DeAngelis Buick somehow held fast against all this decay–renewal tumult, even as its customers, the children of the Hungarian, Italian, and Jewish immigrants who'd settled the neighborhood in the early twentieth century, forsook the inner city for split-levels and neocolonials in the former farmlands of the "other" Brunswicks, North, South, and East. The six DeAngelis brothers and their partner brother-in-law, known collectively as the Seven Thieves, were Old World guys whose American-dream optimism buffed up the place and kept it shiny; they'd emigrated from a village outside Rome ("the other side," as my father put it), started out in bicycles, moved up to Nashes, and finally to Buicks and prosperity. My father, the son of another immigrant, a baker from Poland, was a kindred spirit. Shortly after his return from service in Korea in '54, he answered a "Salesman Wanted" ad in the paper, was hired on the spot by the DeAngelises, and immediately demonstrated a facility for finding good homes for the Specials, Centurys, Supers, and Roadmasters on the floor. He was anointed sales manager in '57, when he was just twenty-six. Over the decades, his fame and his customer following grew and made him a wanted man, forever courted and flattered by other car dealers, who were eager to lure him from the DeAngelises' relatively small inner-city showroom to the airier, bigger, newer dealerships on the white-flight highways out of town. But

Kamp resisted—he and DeAngelis Buick were synonymous. In their vestigial wonderland in a fraying neighborhood, Seymour and the Seven Thieves kept up appearances and ideals, championing cars as a means to a better life.

By the time I became a sentient human being, at the dawn of the 1970s, the Moskowitz-Summers-Abril-Kamp team was a veteran group, in place for a decade. I had no idea that I was witnessing the beginning of the end of something, namely, my father's favorite time in the car business, and that over the next ten or fifteen years Mr. Buick would endure some rough patches.

The thing about America's being a car culture is, every time this culture undergoes a tectonic shift, car families like ours get knocked around and thrown to the carpet. The energy crisis of 1973 was one of those times. I remember idling in fumey gas lines, and I vaguely registered the TV reports of the OPEC oil embargo, but it wasn't until Dad delivered the shocking news—that he was leaving the car business and taking a sales job at his friend's sporting-goods company—that I understood its immediate ramifications. As Dad explained, he'd been accustomed to selling twenty, thirty cars a month. Now he was struggling to sell six or seven. His loyal clientele, stuck in those gas lines and hurting for cash themselves, were putting off their new-car purchases or, apostasy of apostasies, buying Japanese compacts. The energy crisis introduced me to the concept of parental fallibility. I couldn't help but notice how strangely downcast my parents were as we opened our Chanukah presents in 1973, me not quite understanding why they considered it a comedown for us to receive "just" colored pencils and new jean jackets. What I did understand was how weird it felt to have to ride around in a used car like everyone else.

In '74, with the energy crisis in remission, my father returned to

DeAngelis, happily reporting to us that the gas-guzzling Electra 225s were "big as ever, like nothing happened." But six years later came another jolt: I overheard a friend of my father's asking him, "So, Seymour, what's it like to go from working for the Seven Thieves to working for an A-rab?" Thus did I learn that the DeAngelises were selling out to Richie Malouf, a Lebanese American who'd been in the car business in Central Jersey for almost as long as my father. With his pompadour, mustache, and visually assaultive plaid jackets, Richie looked more like your central-casting car salesman than the Sinatra-natty DeAngelises, but to his credit he respected Mr. Buick and asked him to stay on.

Nevertheless, the change of ownership, and Richie's desecration of that gorgeous art deco showroom with rec-room veneer paneling, marked the end of the charmed, tinsel-and-bunting world in which my father had come of professional age. Cut loose from his DeAngelis moorings, jostled awake from his pleasant '50s dream, my father discovered that it was morning in America and decided, in the parlance of the Reagan era, to *go for it*. For years, Ray Catena, the luxury-car magnate, the ultimate big shot of the Central Jersey auto trade, had been after Dad, imploring him to come on board at Catena's Mercedes dealership and make the big bucks he so richly deserved. Over and over, Dad had turned Catena down. But in 1983, he relented. Like George Bailey lowering himself into the sunken chair across from Mr. Potter's desk, my father entered Catena's office and sat silent as the maestro put on his show, flipping through the pay stubs of his Mercedes salesmen, noting aloud that these guys made twice what Dad made as a Buick sales manager. Seriously, what was he waiting for?

But Catena's staff was mostly younger guys, a generation younger than my father, with foul mouths and Mamet tics; they didn't appreciate collegiality, and they sure as hell didn't care for Mr. Buick, with his nice manners and one degree of separation from every human being in Central Jersey. He was out of there in less than a year.

Dad, worldlier and sadder, returned to Buicks, his true love. He got old with them, becoming a granddad as Buicks became grand-dad cars, no longer the dream luxury objects of sharp young guys on the make. And he began to wear down. Late in 1984, he suffered a heart attack and missed a few weeks of work. I was with him in his room at the Robert Wood Johnson hospital when who should come calling but Norman Miller of Miller's on the Mall, jovial and schmoozy in his shorty gown, in for bypass surgery—the two former WCTC merchant-personalities, reunited in the cardio ward by the *tsuris* of keeping up with the ever-mutating world of retail. Norman chatted with us for a while and then bade us farewell. He died on the operating table a few days later.

Seymour healed and still did okay saleswise. But while he had al-ways prided himself on his ability to sell cars to any member of any ethnic group, he was palpably frustrated at his inability to forge an emotional connection with the latest immigrants to make their mark in heterogeneous Central Jersey: the Indians from the Gujarat region, whose numbers were swelling the populations of Edison and Woodbridge. "They don't want to make any conversation," he said forlornly when I visited him one day. "They just get right down to business. [Indian accent] 'I want veddy—goot—deal!' "

But this had to be the capper: His urban-professional son—who had reaped the benefits of his father's Old World ethos, which dic-tated that the material benefits and advanced degrees should be de-ferred to the next generation; who had seen his father work five days and three nights a week, including Saturdays, so that his child would have the freedom to pursue a life of the mind and get paid to think up clever thoughts from the comfiness of a Herman Miller er-gonomic chair—chose, in an appalling act of demographic confor-mity, to make his first car purchase . . . a Volvo.

Dad didn't take the news well. In fact, he tried to kibosh the deal, accusing the Connecticut salesman over the phone of swindling me, and attempted to hook me up with one of his used-car buddies in New Jersey. It was awful, fraught, even harder than when I had to tell him I wasn't marrying a Jewish girl.

But he got over it; the very personality and compassion that made him Mr. Buick precluded him from holding a grudge. (He grew to respect the Volvo and love the bride.) That was one of the things in which I took solace when he died in 2008, at the age of seventy-seven: our utter lack of unresolved "issues," of "if only" scenarios.

Well, perhaps there is one. To my surprise, I haven't lost the Buick pride that was instilled in me in childhood. I've found myself again coveting those boattail Riviera coupes and eternal Electras, both for how they look (fantastic, still) and, I suppose, for what they evoke: that safe, strong world of dads going about their dad business in dad style. They're still out there, these jumbos, in vintage showrooms and on eBay auctions, but I'm gun-shy about actually consummating any deal. What I really want—though I know perfectly well that it's too late—is to buy a Buick from Seymour Kamp.

✳ ✳ ✳

David Kamp is a longtime contributing editor for *Vanity Fair* and the author of, among other books, *The United States of Arugula* and *The Rock Snob's Dictionary*. He began his career at the satirical magazine *Spy*. He grew up in New Jersey, the son of a car-salesman father and microbiologist mother. While the awesomeness of his parents was never in doubt, he has only recently come around to the awesomeness of New Jersey.

christy and teddy

by Kambri Crews

MOM SPOKE CLEARLY. SO CLEARLY, IN fact, that you wouldn't even guess that she was deaf. But if she said a word with multiple s's, you could tell. For fun, I tricked her into saying them.

"Hey Mama, what state's next to Alabama?"

"Missssssissssssssippi," she'd say, sounding like she had been to the dentist and the hiss was waiting for the Novocain to wear off.

I think sometimes it embarrassed her, but I loved it. I loved when Mom said Mississippi.

I was seven years old in 1978 when my family moved from Houston into a trailer off a dirt road in Montgomery, Texas. It was just me and my older brother Kyle—two hearing children living with deaf parents. Settling into our new home, I emptied a box onto our dining-room table and sifted through report cards, yearbooks, and glossy black-and-white pictures.

"Mama, what's this stuff?"

"Those are my souvenirs from when I was a girl."

I traced the letters on the cover of a yearbook and asked, "What's Will Rogers?"

"A hearing school I went to before I had to go to deaf school," she signed. "It was named after the famous cowboy."

"You went to a *hearing* school?"

"Yep! That meant I could live at home with my parents all year. Look here," she signed, pointing to a picture of her amid a group of young girls dressed in gingham-checked uniforms. "I was on the pep squad. We had pom-poms and went to all the football games. I even remember our cheer, 'Hey! Hey! Whatdya say? Bobcats get that ball away!' "

I was mesmerized. Mom looked like Sandra Dee from *Grease*.

"If you went to hearing school, then how did you meet Daddy?"

As Mom got older, her hearing deteriorated and her grades slipped. "I sat in the front row and tried to keep up but I couldn't. My best friend and my sister were at the deaf school anyway."

Dad and his twin brother, Frank, were the only boys out of ten children. Together they lived on a farm in the Dust Bowl of Bowlegs, Oklahoma. Even though his parents were hearing, Dad, like three of his sisters, was born deaf. But Frank and five other sisters could hear perfectly fine. With no history of hearing loss in preceding generations or those that would follow, some might call it a fluke. Dad considered it an unmistakable "Up Yours" from the Man in Charge.

Dad's family didn't know sign language and used homemade hand signals to communicate the basics. When Dad saw them talking to one another—lips moving, jaws opening back and forth—he joined in by moving his lips and tongue with great exaggeration. No sound came out of his mouth; he was a puppet missing his ventriloquist.

When Dad turned five he was sent to the Oklahoma School for the Deaf. He lived in dorms for the entire school year, going home only on holidays and summer vacation.

If Mom was Sandy, Dad was Danny Zuko, and then some. He was athletic, good looking, and had a bad reputation. His smooth skin was bronzed and his dark, shiny hair slicked back. In every picture, he posed with classic cars, his arm slung around the shoulder of different teenage girls. He wore tight white T-shirts, jeans with the cuffs rolled up, and black leather dress shoes.

Mom was a sophomore when she enrolled at the deaf school. "Your daddy picked on me from day one. He told everyone I wasn't a natural redhead and dyed my hair. When I wasn't looking, he emptied a full shaker of salt in my milk. I took a few big gulps and swallowed a huge chunk.

"Your daddy laughed and said, 'I just thought you'd take a sip and it would taste funny. I didn't think you'd guzzle it!' Well, that night, I got so sick. I vomited and coughed up blood so they took me to the infirmary. My very first night! Your daddy came to visit and told me he was sorry. From then on, he pestered me to go out with him but I told him, 'No, I'm already dating Garland.' "

Garland was a senior and Mom's first boyfriend. She pointed him out in the yearbook and her voice got dreamy. "He was an all-pro football and basketball player, six foot four with blond hair and blue eyes. Everybody loved him, teachers, my mom and dad, everybody." She shielded her mouth as she whispered in a singsong, "He took my virginity.

"But," she went on, sighing, "your daddy wouldn't take no for an answer. When I went to get my books, he jumped in front of my locker and asked me again. If I bent down for a sip from the water fountain, he stepped in between to ask me again. This went on for three or four *months*!"

The deck was stacked against him. Three different teachers warned Mom about my father, one emphatically signing, "Don't go with him. He's a bad boy. He's a sadist!" But Teddy Crews was not to be denied, and eventually Mom relented.

"I told him, 'If I go to the movies with you—*as a friend*—then you can't bother me anymore.' "

One date with Dad was all it took, and Garland was kicked to the curb. Judging by Mom's far-off gaze and wrinkled chin, it was a decision she lamented, for Mom and Dad went together like an open flame in a fireworks stand.

Mom stared at the photo in silence. The girl in the picture looked so happy. She was popular, the best-dressed girl on the pep squad, and she had a romance worthy of the silver screen. After a moment, Mom snapped out of it. "But if I had stayed with Garland, you and Kyle would never have been born. Who knows, maybe I'd be living in Missssssississsssssppi."

I loved it when Mom said Mississippi.

✳ ✳ ✳

Kambri Crews is a publicist and producer specializing in stand-up comedy. She can be seen at various comedy and storytelling shows in New York City, where she lives with her husband, comedian Christian Finnegan. Her memoir *Love, Daddy*, detailing her life with with deaf parents and the fallout from her father's homicidal tendencies, is forthcoming from Random House. Read more at LoveDaddy.org.

joe and patricia

by Tom McAllister

JOE HAD BEEN STALKING PATRICIA FOR WEEKS. Not so much in the weirdly aggressive and mildly felonious manner of romantic comedies, but really in the gentlest way possible. Still, a risky strategy, because at what point does the stalker, once discovered, get to explain himself? How likely is the stalkee to listen to him, especially if his first words are *It's not what you think*? But he just didn't know what else to do.

A man without any specific direction, he was not caught up in the counterculture, not permitted to join his friends in Vietnam due to a bone disorder in his feet. Stuck somewhere in the middle of everything. Floundering. At twenty-one, he'd already begun his fourth new career, delivering mail, which was okay but not particularly satisfying in any way. Life had to be about more than passing the time until you could go home.

Work does not define a man unless he lets it; sometimes Joe worried he was allowing himself to be defined as The Mailman, this mustached young fellow who would nod politely to the neighbors every day and grow old along with them, delivering first housewarming cards, then mortgage statements, then tuition bills, then postcards from their children in exotic places, then advertisements for hearing aids and orthopedic shoes, then Social Security checks, until one day they all retired or died at the same time and a new kid took over the route and the world continued as if Joe had never existed. They lived in Manayunk, a Northwest Philly neighborhood that could make anyone claustrophobic, the sharply rising hills like walls. Gossip fueled the residents the way sunlight fuels plants; the neighbors, deeply rooted in their own homes, energized by rumor and hearsay, compulsively leaned toward it, pressing ears against walls and leaving the windows open at night, just in case something happened outside. And yet, few people knew anything about Joe, beyond that he was a good son, his father drank a little too much, and his mother was as close to saintly as anyone could be. They didn't know he liked to hole himself up in his bedroom with sci-fi novels for whole days, or that seeing *Alfred Hitchcock Presents* on TV in 1962 had engendered a lifelong love of both television and mysteries. The neighbors knew he liked to cruise in his 1970 Chrysler Sport Fury, but they didn't realize he *loved* it, or that rolling down Ridge Avenue—lid down, windows up—was about more than showing off; it was about indulging himself and reminding the world *Yes, I am alive*, if only for a moment, and it was also about reminding himself that as long as he could wrangle this roaring beast around sharp curves and up the neighborhood's hills—without power steering, he looked like a sea captain battling a nor'easter—he always had the potential of taking off one day, driving until he was out of gas and cash, settling in some new place where he could be anybody. A uniquely American dream—the open road, the self-sufficient loner, all of that. He wanted, sometimes, to be a cowboy. He wanted to ride.

The day he first saw Patricia, he was leaning on his car on Cotton Street, back to the road, cigarette pinched between his lips. Two of his friends—Denny and Paul—stood with him, Denny complaining about work while stabbing his own cigarette out against the wall of his house. They were going to head out to a movie, maybe, or play pool, or maybe just drive. Young, they had energy to spare. Restless, they needed to be in motion, buzzing, worried that the moment they slowed down the world would move on without them.

Behind Joe, a storm door slammed shut. A metal trash can clanged and scraped on the sidewalk. Joe's friends stopped talking, and he turned just in time to see her, dragging the can behind her. She looked up at the boys, her eyes meeting Joe's for less than a second, and then she turned away, disappeared back into her house, the storm door slamming behind her. Denny pounded a cigarette out of the pack, demanded a light, and then said, "We got to get out of here." Paul agreed and hopped into Joe's car. Denny pounded on the horn. "Let's go," he said.

"Maybe we should hang around here a while," Joe said, still eyeing the house across the street.

Here's what Joe saw when Patricia hauled the trash to the curb: a girl with the kindest eyes in the world. A girl whose bashful smile radiated enough warmth to melt an iceberg. A girl he needed to see again, if only to remind himself of what it's like to be stunned. Like most twenty-one-year-olds, Joe had read just enough and learned just enough to think he knew everything, and so it was important to embrace clarifying moments like this.

A week later, Joe parked across the street again, leaned on the wall facing Patricia's house, struck his best James Dean pose as he smoked against the wall, and waited, his friends at his side. Around eight o'clock, she dragged the cans outside again. He followed her eyes. If she would let him, he would never stop looking into them. He wished he could write as well as he could read; then he would write her a poem, in which he analogized and similied and metaphored her eyes and her smile until she had no choice but to love him. If ever given the opportunity, he would say her eyes reminded him of the morning sky, the way they practically exploded with color and possibility. When she reached the curb, he waved. She did not wave back, did not even seem to notice him.

Joe lived only a few blocks away from Patricia, but had never seen her before. He was a member of the neighborhood's Irish parish and she belonged to the Polish parish at the end of her street, and so their paths rarely crossed. If not for his friendship with Denny and Paul, who'd also grown up on Cotton Street, he would probably never have seen her.

Since that first trash night, Joe had gathered some basic information, mostly from Denny and Paul: She preferred to be called Pat, she was eighteen and lived with her parents and younger sister, graduated from Roxborough High, and now attended nursing school. Once, in high school, she and a group of friends had waited at the airport for Herman's Hermits, screaming and waving signs and (possibly) fainting.

Paul was not there for the third week of the vigil. Denny and Joe stood in their usual spots across the street, and Denny asked Joe, "What's the big deal about her anyway?" Joe explained that even though they'd never spoken, he could tell she was the type of woman you marry, kind and compassionate, tender and intelligent. Besides, Joe explained, she was very pretty. Denny flicked his cigarette into the street. "She is cute," he said.

When she dragged the trash out that night, her father watched from the doorway, arms crossed. Joe did not wave. Pat did not wave. They did not make eye contact.

Joe had been on a few dates in his life, but wasn't particularly popular, and since he went to an all-boy high school, it was not uncommon to go weeks without even conversing with a girl. Frankly, he was at a disadvantage when trying to attract girls his age. Young women wanted excitement and adventure and maybe some danger; he didn't believe in drugs or excessive drinking or even profanity, and his chief qualities were that he was reliable and honest, the kinds of things many women don't look for until they're forty and divorced. He liked wordplay—crossword puzzles, puns, and palindromes—and compelling conversation. Few girls even humored him once the puns started.

So, no serious girlfriends, no prospects on the horizon, he understood the ostensible appeal of dating but, pre-Pat, had never himself been infatuated like others had. Life wasn't lonely, necessarily, because he had friends and he had family, but it wasn't fulfilled either. Something missing, always.

He started cruising down Cotton Street in the car more frequently. Parked at Denny's house to wax and wash the Fury, radio cranked to Dave Herman's rock show. Stopped reading and watching TV so that he could spend his spare time in her orbit. One day, finally, they stood face-to-face, an accident, Joe—not looking for her this time—on his mail route and Pat walking home from classes. He almost didn't recognize her, but then the eyes, the soft smile. Pat putting her head down and pretending not to see him. "Wait," he said, and she stopped. "I'm Joe."

She said she knew. She'd seen him around.

He offered her a ride home, and she said her father probably wouldn't like that. "He doesn't really like you," she said. On the other hand, she *was* exhausted, and Joe seemed like a nice enough guy, she said.

He assured her he was nice, as long as she gave him a chance.

A minute later, they were in the truck, rumbling down Shurs Lane, and she asked him if he liked being a mailman. He said he didn't, not really.

It was a short ride, maybe five minutes. In front of her house, engine idling, he asked if he could see her again. On a real date. She said she would think about it, and then she added, "See you on trash day."

He gave her gifts—flowers, cards, stuffed animals, earrings. Money he would have spent maintaining the Fury diverted toward her, toward dinners and movie tickets and anything she wanted. She accompanied him to the smoky pool hall, even though she was bored. He liked taking her because he was good at pool, had his own cue, could process the angles and the geometry almost instantaneously; call him Manayunk Fats. Besides his car, his prowess at pool was maybe his only attribute that could be described as *cool*, and so he wanted to perform for her. Some sort of modern mating dance. After a few trips to the pool hall, she told him he didn't need to keep trying to impress her, but he said that's all he ever wanted to do.

She tolerated his puns and his wordplay.

She convinced her parents to give him a chance, and he seemed to grow on them.

She loved his mother and his mother loved Pat.

She didn't mind spending quiet nights at home watching television while her friends were out at the bar with fake IDs and endless possibilities.

She twirled his curly hair around her index finger.

She leaned into his chest when she was cold, and she told him he should smile more, and she let him hold the door for her, and she made him feel like they were the only two people in the room.

She kissed him when he arrived and when he left, and it was so sweet that he wanted to leave and return thirty times a day.

✳ ✳ ✳

Tom McAllister's first book—*Bury Me in My Jersey: A Memoir of My Father, Football, and Philly*—was published by Villard in 2010. He is a graduate of the Iowa Writers' Workshop and La Salle University in Philadelphia. A lecturer in the English Department at Temple University, he lives with his wife and two dogs in New Jersey.

ron and sherry

by Rebecca Serle

THEY WALK UP THE TINY STEPS TO HER ATTIC. It is so quiet she thinks maybe he can hear her heart beating. "I can't believe you really like them," she says. "I haven't been able to sell a single one!" She realizes she is shrieking a little and doesn't say anything more. *Is this a date?* she wonders over and over. He is silent behind her, a little nervous. Every now and again he will remark about the weather but there isn't much to say: It is the beginning of winter and it is cold.

His name is Ron and he owns a small clothing store in downtown Philadelphia. Her name is Sherry and she sells poodle scarves. Well, she designs poodle scarves. Other things, too, of course but right now, because she cannot give these poodle scarves away, she hasn't really been able to afford to move her business along. She has piles of poodle scarves, buckets and boxes of poodle scarves, all in various colors. Some are pink with white poodles, others are green with black poodles. None will sell. This man, this silly, nerdy, stumbling man bought her poodle scarves last week and now he is back for more.

"Flew right off the rack," he tells her.

"Really?" she says, eyeing him carefully. "*My* poodle scarves?"

"Yes," he says, "people really like them."

They walk up the stairs to the attic and she points around the room.

"Take your pick," she says. "I can't give them away."

He goes over to a box filled with white scarves with yellow poodles.

"I like these," he says. "You're very talented."

"Thank you," she says, "but the poodles weren't a very good idea. I really thought they'd sell, that they'd be different. Oh well."

She takes a seat on a box and watches him sort through her designs. He is cute, she thinks, not too tall and not too short. And he looks kind. He has a big head of black, curly hair and wears funny clothing. The last time she saw him, well, when she met him, he had on a shirt that was too small in the wrists. It made him look like a character out of a Shakespearean play or something. Now he is wearing a blue shirt and slacks. He looks nice, important even. She thinks that maybe he doesn't dress like this every day, maybe he dressed up today for her. She imagines him in the same outfit sitting behind a big oak desk. She thinks he is smart, that maybe he wants to do a lot of things with his life that he hasn't yet.

"So," he says, pulling out a pink poodle scarf, "what else do you design?"

"Oh lots of thing," she says. "I make the most beautiful denim jackets and pins. You really should see my pins. I collect antique buttons for them." She goes to a small dresser in the far corner of the attic and pulls out a little container. She shakes it and it makes a sound like a maraca. She opens the lid and goes over to him. "See?" she says, taking out a round, flat, gold button. "This one is from the eighteenth century."

"Very nice," he says.

"I make cufflinks with them sometimes," she says. "I could make you a pair." He opens his mouth and then closes it again. She blushes and looks away. "I mean, if you wanted them."

"Very much," he says, "thank you."

He looks at her then for a very long time. She thinks he might even take off his glasses, he is looking at her so long. Again she wonders: *Is this a date?* No, no no no. The man owns a store and she is a designer and he called so he can get more merchandise. *But poodle scarves?* she says to herself.

"Well?" she says, because someone needs to speak. "What do you think?"

"I'll take them all," he says, looking away.

"What?" she says.

"All the poodle scarves," he says.

"But there are hundreds," she says. "You cannot possibly sell hundreds." He looks hurt when she says it and she tries again. "I just mean they have been selling so terribly, I wouldn't want you to get stuck with a bunch of scarves you couldn't sell."

"Don't worry," he says. "I really like them."

He has a car downstairs, a small beat-up red car where the paint is cracked in places. She helps him and together they carry the boxes of poodle scarves one by one down the steps of the attic through her small little cottage house and outside. They load the car up from top to bottom with poodle scarves.

"That's the last of it," she says, closing a car door. He nods and takes out his wallet.

"How much do I owe you?" he says.

She fidgets with her fingers and looks up at the sky.

"Three hundred dollars," she says.

She sees him wince a little but then he takes out his checkbook.

"Would it be possible for me to pay you in installments?" he says. "You see, the store is just going through some renovations right now and things—" She puts a hand on his arm and cuts him off.

"That would be fine," she says.

He writes her a check for sixty dollars.

"I promise to give you more soon," he says, "I really do." He is looking at her again and so sincere she thinks he might cry.

"Are you hungry?" she asks.

"What?" he says. "Oh, sorry, well, yes, sort of."

"Would you like to go to dinner?" she asks. He looks puzzled for a moment, like he isn't sure what she is asking. "I know a very good place around the corner, they make great pasta." He doesn't say anything, just looks at the check in his hands. "You've been so kind," she says, "it's on me." He looks up and shakes his head.

"All this time I've been thinking of a way to ask you out," he says, "and you beat me to it." She smiles and so does he.

"I think we should walk," she says. "There doesn't appear to be much room in the car."

"Aren't you cold?" he asks.

She holds up her index finger and darts into the car. She rummages around until she has found it: an eggshell scarf with a turquoise poodle stitched on.

"This should keep me warm," she says, taking his arm.

Ron likes to say that three hundred dollars was a cheap price to pay for a date with my mother. He never sold the poodle scarves, not a single one, but two weeks later my father moved into that small cottage with the empty attic and six years later they were married.

Today there is a box that sits on the top shelf of my mother's closet. It only has one item in it and while I have never asked to borrow it (there was a reason no one ever bought those poodle scarves) I do like to look at that eggshell scarf every once in a while. When I do I remember something about love.

✳ ✳ ✳

Rebecca Serle is a New York City–based writer and a Huffington Post columnist. Her first novel is due out in Summer 2012.

chuck and debra

by Alex Blagg

BACK IN THE LATE '70S, before I was born, Chuck and Debra Blagg (whom I would come to know and love as "my parents") appeared as contestants on seven episodes of a new game show called *Family Feud.* My existence is a direct result of this.

Both products of pretty dysfunctional families (which would maybe turn out to be a blessing?), my parents married young, seeming to find in each other both a safe harbor from their past and the possibility for a new and better future. They joined the air force together as a way to pay for college. By 1978, they were both officers, living meagerly but happily at Vandenberg Air Force Base outside Santa Barbara, where they were stationed.

One weekend they decided to take a low-budget vacation to nearby Los Angeles, joined by a few of my aunts and uncles who had driven down from Sacramento to meet them. As my family consists almost entirely of lovable dorks (a personal brand my parents still employ to this day), they certainly weren't "showbiz types" in search of (or likely even aware of) the swinging "coke bumps and casual sex with Warren Beatty in a booth at Morton's" aspects of the late-'70s Hollywood tourism experience.

There was, however, enough showbiz in their blood for them to work up the courage to visit Studio 54 at ABC Television Center to go on an impromptu audition for *Family Feud,* which one of my dad's helicopter pilot buddies had recently told them about. The latest television confection from legendary producer-creator Merv Griffin, this show was apparently looking for teams of five people, who were related to each other by blood or marriage, for a game hosted by the awesomely pervy Richard Dawson that would test people's ability to predict popular opinion on a variety of subjects in a fun, fast-paced, family-against-family competition.

After managing to endure a series of mock-*Feuds* with other fiercely competitive fame-seeking families, and desperate producers mercilessly encouraging them to be funnier, happier, and more enthusiastic, my family emerged victorious, and were selected as combatants for an actual *Feud* on actual television.

Even at first glance, the Blaggs were formidable competitors. My mother and father honored their country by appearing in their air force dress uniforms (they are certain this played a major part in their casting success), with my dad's sweet mustache and Mom's playfully feathered hair serving as subtle indicators that they were patriots, but not total squares. The rest of the family was rounded out by my uncle Fred, a suave car salesman in tinted '70s specs, his wife, Lori, and my aunt Dee Dee, who was utterly unable to contain her enthusiasm and would spaz out at so much as a sideways glance from big Dick Dawson (the producers loved her).

The Blaggs won the first show they appeared on, but failed to increase their haul in the Fast Money round. The next day, they lost show number two and, after their brief flirtation with *Feud* fame, returned to the air force base with little more than a pretty good story and the novelty of getting to be on television.

A few months later, when their episodes finally aired, my parents and their friends noticed that Richard Dawson had accepted a clearly incorrect answer from the winning team in the second show. My mother wrote a letter to the show's producers, pointing out the error, and a few weeks later received a surprising call from the producers, who acknowledged the mistake and invited them back on the show for another chance.

They went on to appear in five more episodes, winning the first four. These old reruns can be seen on the Game Show Network to this day, and my father, who is now a high school teacher, has an annual tradition of showing a VHS tape of the shows to his class (whose favorite part is invariably the moment when my dad, in his full pilot regalia, looks purposefully into the camera and states, without irony, "I'd like to say hello to my unit."). When all was said and done, the Blaggs departed with lots of fancy prizes (a cutting-edge cassette player!), lifelong memories of being pawed at by Richard Dawson (I still wince when I see the way he manhandled my mother), and cash winnings in excess of sixteen thousand dollars.

After splitting up the money, my parents used their portion to landscape their front yard and finally take the slightly higher-budget vacation they could now afford, to Club Med in Playa Blanca Mexico, where they enjoyed a carefree week of margaritas, forbidden dancing, and wild abandon. Nine months later, I was born.

Now, I know it's crazy to think about the endless variables, conditions, and circumstances that must be met for even the most mundane event to have taken place, let alone something as monumental (to me, at least) as my own birth. And not to sound like a college freshman pondering the deepest "What does it all mean?" mysteries of existence late at night after smoking his first joint, but for my entire life, I have been haunted by the knowledge that I am a product of a 1970s television game show whose entire existence hinges upon my parents' charm, tenacity, and virtuosic ability to shout out free-associated answers to questions such as, "What kind of items might one find in a laundry room?"

Survey says: My parents were awesome.

✳ ✳ ✳

Alex Blagg is a writer and comedian whose work has appeared on Google. He now lives in Los Angeles with his wife, their dog, and a Twitter.

bob and leslie

by Bex Schwartz

MY PARENTS MET IN COLLEGE when they were very young and got married right after my dad graduated. My mom always claimed that her friends had been trying to set her up with this engineer guy named "Schwartz" for months, but she was dating his RA and wasn't particularly interested. Then the March on Washington happened and all the hippies at Barnard and Columbia schlepped down to D.C.—except the engineers, who had a major exam the next day, and my mother, because she had sprained her ankle (and wasn't, truth be told, all that much of a hippie).

Whenever we would get my parents to talk about their hippie days, my dad would wave us off and my mom would say that she could never be a real hippie because she was too uncomfortable going without a bra. Then she would tell us stories about my dad's long hair and how his roommate was beaten by a cop during the 1968 riots and ended up losing a spleen. For the record, my dad wore an armband but wasn't militant, mostly because he was way into esoteric folk music, and, man, those cats didn't want to fight. And then my dad would get angry because he wanted them to get married barefoot in Sheep Meadow in Central Park and my mom's family forced them to get married in my mom's synagogue in Poughkeepsie. My dad wanted a be-in and they ended up at Beth El.

But back to the fateful day on campus . . . My dad was coerced into going to a party, and there was my mom, sitting on the floor with her crutches. I never heard this part of the story until right after my mom died, and we were talking about her funeral service with the rabbi. The rabbi asked my dad how they had met, and when he knew that she was going to be the woman he would marry. My dad paused. "I knew right away," he said. "Leslie was a real one-er."

My mom used to describe their courtship—how they would stay up all night eating Screaming Yellow Zonkers until *The New York Times* hit the newsstands, so they could read the paper in the wee hours of the morning and do the crossword puzzle in bed. According to my mom, there was never a romantic sort of wedding proposal—my dad just turned to her one day and said, "So, how about it?" I'm not sure if this is apocryphal because my mother was also the queen of making up anecdotes to support her claims, but it seems about right.

My parents were married for seven years before they had me— because they wanted to wait until they had enough money that I wouldn't have to be a baby sleeping in a dresser drawer. And they were amazing parents. They stood up for me throughout the course of my most losery years—telling me the girls who were mean to me were just stupid, confirming that the boys who didn't like me were just immature. After college, I went on vacation with my theater troupe and ate mushrooms and ended up calling them, convinced I had seen the truth of the universe, and thanking them for raising me to be "smart and intellectual." My mom wept and told me that I was finally back from being a sullen teen and my dad just told me what books I should read next. In fact, he and I share the same taste in books, and he once gave me our cherished copy of *Fool on the Hill* by Matt Ruff inside of which he'd dog-eared the page where the father wanted his daughter to be a lesbian just to be unconventional. (I am strictly dickly these days, but at the time I was fresh out of Wesleyan and questioning my sexuality and that tiny dog-ear meant acceptance more than any conversation could ever imply.)

As I got older, my parents and I became even closer. My mom talked me through the agita of my first real relationship with a man who was afraid of commitment. My dad talked me through job confusion and how to deal with friends who were turning into vampires (metaphorically, of course—this was long before *Twilight*). After the Winter Olympics, my dad decided to change his name to Yevgeni and I bought him a Russian officer's hat and gave him a card that said he was my best friend. In fact, we were the closest we had ever been because email was so much easier than talking on the phone. My mom was probably hurt and jealous of my closeness with my father. At the time, she and I were too alike, so we bickered. She had no idea that *she* was really my best friend in the universe.

During my mom's illness, I watched my dad develop a nurturing side that I'd never really seen. He bought her a Snuggie and asked me to pick up scarves and hats when her hair fell out. He tried to get her to eat when she refused, and made a continuous stream of milk shakes enforced with protein powder. He stopped traveling for work and started coming home early to spend time with her. I spent weekends with them and gave my mom a spa-pedicure when it seemed like she was doing better. The day she died, we were unprepared. We knew she was very sick, but the doctors said we had a couple of years. My dad went into the bathroom and found her passed out on the floor. When he woke her, she was incoherent. My dad and my aunt called an ambulance and the doctors at the hospital said it was bad and that we should start thinking about hospice. Mere moments after my brother and I got to the ER, my mom slipped into a coma. Less than an hour later, she was gone.

My dad and I drove back to their house and the first thing we did was open all the windows and gather up all her blankets and pillows and nightgowns to throw into the washing machine. And then we called about a thousand people because my mom had so many friends. And then we sat on the couch and cried. "In this world full of terrible, horrible people, why do the good ones have to go?" my dad wailed. "Why are Bush and Cheney still alive and Leslie is dead?"

That's my dad, still a hippie, still wanting to right the wrongs of the world and let good triumph over evil. Their fortieth wedding anniversary would have been next year. I'm a Universal Life Church minister and I had already started the preparations for them to renew their vows in Sheep Meadow in Central Park. Maybe my brother and I will take my dad there for a private be-in instead.

✳ ✳ ✳

Bex Schwartz is a writer-director and a regular comediator (comedian-commentator) about all things pop culture on various TV channels. She spends most of her free time deconstructing reality shows with friends and thinking about pandas. Bex loves her awesome dad and misses her mom more than anything in the multiverse.

gerry and maddy

by Dave Itzkoff

WHAT YOU HAVE TO REMEMBER IS THAT there was a time when Michael Caine was not just a dignified elder states-man of the cinema, but a roguishly handsome screen idol who could charm his way even through a movie like *Alfie,* in which he talks directly to the screen, refers to ladies as birds, makes cuckolds of married men, and puts a lover in a position where she's forced to have an abortion. He could do all of this and still inspire a classic Burt Bacharach song of the same title—a song so pervasive and infectious in its own right that when my grandmother became the proud owner of a purebred Airedale in 1966, there was only one name she could think to give him: Alfie.

This news was hardly of much consequence to my parents, who had just gotten married the previous year, unless you want to draw the correlation between my grandmother's adoption of a new dog and the departure of her twenty-six-year-old son from the Itzkoff family homestead. What was understandably most important to them was that they begin to forge their own path and create their own family, and if a fifty-five-year-old bubbeh-in-waiting from the Bronx wanted to take in a dog that, at its maturation, would be as heavy and as tall on its hind legs as she, there was no need for them to talk her out of a decision that had no bearing on the lives they were about to lead.

For my mother and father the next decade was all about freedom from responsibility and not being obligated to anyone except each other. Their lives were as boundless as their capacity to want, and what they wanted was to take road trips from New York to Mexico, go marlin fishing in Florida, sit five rows back from the stage when the Grateful Dead played the Fillmore East, and sort their stems and seeds on the covers of newly purchased Elton John albums that no one knew yet were classics.

They graduated from an apartment in Yonkers to a three-room house in Edgewater, New Jersey, to a deluxe high-rise in a pristine Manhattan building, and when my mother felt, after these ten nomadic, hedonistic, satisfying years, that what she wanted now was a child, my father complied with her tearful entreaties and they produced a son. When they liked him so much that they wanted a second child, they had a daughter eighteen months later.

Whether or not they wanted Alfie, they soon ended up with him, too.

My grandmother started getting sick and was frequently traveling to New York University Hospital for kidney dialysis treatments. Her only options for Alfie were to put him in a kennel for frequent, extended periods of time, which everyone understood was inhumane, or to make my parents the provisional caretakers of her one hundred-pound mangle of hair, teeth, and bones. Besides which, one of her daughters was too fancy to keep a dog in her house and the other was too unreliable, and my father lived closest to the hospital, anyway. It may not have been what my father or mother wanted, but they knew it was what needed to be done.

Added to the zero years that my mother had grown up around pets, the time that my father spent in his childhood home growing up with my grandmother's previous dog, a harmless, pocket-sized Irish terrier named Hubba, was hardly adequate preparation for them to raise Alfie alongside two small children in their suddenly claustrophobic Manhattan high-rise. His short, two-syllable name turned out to possess just the right piercing cadence to cause maximum irritation when it was spoken at maximum volume, which was often. Left alone in the apartment for just a few hours, Alfie dug or possibly ate a crater in the wall that went well beneath the paint into the plaster below. Taken for the summer to my parents' Catskills bungalow and set free to roam the grounds, Alfie ate the garbage and was sprayed by a skunk. One day he returned from his daily wandering clutching between his teeth a wooden plank that was twice as long as he was, and which my parents later deduced had been pried from a telephone pole. When my father would clutch his jaws in his hand and shout, "Alfie Shmigalfie! Alfie Shmigalfie!" the dog seemed to like it.

When Alfie neared his seventeenth birthday, it was my parents who had to make the decision that his remaining days would be best spent at an animal farm and hospital not too far from their Catskills bungalow. They were also the ones who had to take responsibility for explaining to their seven-year-old son that he had died, and to hold him as he cried at the realization that this meant Alfie was gone and never coming back. This made things only slightly easier when my parents had to tell me a few years later that my grandmother had died, too.

But Alfie was not completely gone from our family. Not long after they finished grieving for my grandmother, my parents acquired a small black Airedale puppy of their own, who they invariably named Alfie 2; he grew up and moved with us from Manhattan to our new house in the suburbs of Rockland County. And when Alfie 2 died suddenly while I was on a college trip to London—as my parents explained in a tearful phone call—they buried him in their backyard, and that same weekend took in a new puppy they named Alfie 3.

Alfie 3 came with my parents when they moved from Rockland County to live year-round in the Catskills; they changed their email address to include the phrase "alfie3," and when he was hit and dragged by a car one day on a country road, they spent several thousand dollars to have him fixed up by a veterinary surgeon in Manhattan, just so he could live a couple more years. They asked, half joking, if they could bring him to my wedding, before he had to be put to sleep a few months later.

One summer, not long ago, my parents made a road trip to rural Kentucky, to the breeder who provided them with Alfie 4. (In fact, they made two trips to Kentucky and back—one to choose their new puppy after he was born, and one to pick him up after he'd been weaned from his mother.) This latest Alfie is something of a holy terror, and I hear his name shouted repeatedly in the background whenever I call my parents now, usually followed by the phrase "Stop it!" or "Put that down!" "He's got a good heart," my father usually explains, by way of apology.

My parents have 135 years of life between them, and it is noticeably harder for them to keep up with Alfie 4 than it was with his predecessors. But this is what they want. "It's nice to keep traditions alive," my father says.

Sometimes, in moments when her mind is disposed to unflinching pragmatism, my wife will ask me, "What would ever happen if your parents couldn't take care of Alfie anymore?" Often before I can respond, she will add: "He's *not* becoming our responsibility."

What I usually say in these conversations is: "We'll see."

✳ ✳ ✳

Dave Itzkoff is a reporter on the culture desk of *The New York Times* and the lead contributor to its popular ArtsBeat blog. He is the author of two memoirs for Villard Books, *Cocaine's Son* and *Lads,* and has written for numerous publications, including *GQ, Vanity Fair, Details, Wired, Elle, Spin, The New York Times Book Review,* and *New York* magazine. He lives in New York with his wife, Amy.

david

by Jackie Mancini

MY DAD AND I UNDERSTAND EACH OTHER. We are one and the same: two crazy-brained, wanderlusting, free-spirited peas in a pod. When I visited him in his home in Germany six years ago, I convinced him to let me bring back to America with me fifty photos of him when he was my age (I was twenty-one at the time). There was something about them that made me feel both powerfully nostalgic and surprisingly sad, even though I wasn't alive when any of them were taken. He and I, I realized, are connected in our idealization of the world, of people, of beauty, and of chance. Those pictures sit in a wooden clementine box on my coffee table; they are the first thing people look at when they come over to visit. I'm proud of them; they help explain who I am.

I didn't know my dad for a good chunk of my childhood, so during my formative years when I was becoming a miniature version of him, I didn't realize it. I could see it in my mom's eyes pretty clearly, though. That look of nervous recognition when I would come home from a friend's house with a full head of newly bleached hair, when I would proclaim—at the dinner table—that instead of going to college I wanted to be the next Amelia Earhart, or when I would drive through the night from Virginia to New York to pick up my best friend, then turn around and drive back in time for an 8 AM class. That restless energy—the need to keep my feet moving—for a long time I didn't know where it came from.

After not seeing each other for nearly ten years, my father and I got to know each other again in Germany over bottles of cheap wine, and photographs helped fill in the gaps on both sides. I showed him school pictures, old boyfriends, pictures from punk rock shows. He basically showed me the same, only the schools, girlfriends, and bands were different. Looking at those photographs, hearing the stories, I developed a better understanding of who I was and where I came from. He told me about hitchhiking across America in the backseat of a car, sandwiched between a man clutching a knife under his coat, and another who was a drug-runner for his grandmother. He grew up in the skinniest house in all of Brooklyn. He washed dishes at Nepenthe in Big Sur when it was a mecca for artists, vagabonds, musicians, and travelers. He once traveled around in a bus that was one big bed, in which everyone "cuddled" at night. My dad is insane, but in the very best way possible. In fact, he's my idol (just don't tell my mom, who divorced him when I was three).

Because I know these things about my dad, he's the first one I call when I have a crazy story to tell. I know that if no one else understands or appreciates it, my dad will gasp with delight when I tell him about running down the beach at night in Ocracoke, North Carolina, while bioluminescent zooplankton lit up the sand under my feet. I can hear his smile grow over the telephone lines when I call it "Star Sand"—he understands my language. He, as steeped in metaphor as I am, is one of the only people in my life I don't need to explain myself to. Dad once told me that when my mom was pregnant with me, she was expecting a "skinny Irish boy," a fact, until that point, unbeknownst to me. What she got instead, he said, was a "full-grown Italian woman with hips and heart."

"You must drive her *crazy*," he told me as we sipped our drinks from chipped mugs across his yellow coffee table in his apartment in Hannover. He was right. I did. I do. She loves me unconditionally and fiercely, despite our radical differences.

I tried to calm down, really I did. I was in a stable relationship with someone who was nothing like me, who cherished me; we bought a house, we got dogs. My mother was delighted—she sent me shower curtain rings and we talked about kitchen renovations—we were relating in a way that we never had been able to before. For a while, I was able to put a part of myself to sleep and be happy in that little brick house in a suburb of Richmond, Virginia. Slowly, though, the fever crept inside of me and I found myself buying books about travel, sleeping in tents in the backyard, having vivid dreams about adventures. This fever wasn't inside of him, and so I left that stability to figure out what it is that I wanted. Ultimately, we are who we are.

Now alone, I find that wanderlust, the same one that kept my dad virtually nomadic until he finally settled down in Germany, growing and pushing me to explore places, see things, grow and learn as much as I can. On his birthday this year I called him, and we spent a long time talking about how now, in my mid-twenties, was the time to do what I wanted. And that resonated for me. A few hours later I pulled out Kurt Vonnegut's *Deadeye Dick*, a book I had often eyed but never sat down to read. I sat there in my new, mostly empty apartment, opened the book, and immediately noticed an inscription on the inside cover. Written from my mother to my father on his birthday—to the day—twenty-seven years ago. My mother was just two months' pregnant with me, although she may very well have been unaware.

October 25th, 1982

Dear David,

Happy 34th Birthday. I hope you have enjoyed your Saturn Transit. The years ahead are the best to come.

All my love,
Ann-Marie

Apparently, my father was a space traveler, but I haven't seen any of those photos (yet).

✳ ✳ ✳

Jackie Mancini would love to tie up everything in her apartment into a giant bundle and hit the road in her glimmering, silver Airstream. She's just waiting to find a big enough handkerchief to hold all her typewriters and moldy books. She's also waiting until she actually owns an Airstream. In the meantime, she lives in Richmond, Virginia, in an apartment overlooking the trains, and there are binoculars hanging from her windowsill, so if you happen to pull into Main Street Station, wave.

seymour

by Philip Glist

MY DAD SPENT HIS LIFE WONDERING, *How did I get here?*
How does the editor of the literary magazine at Boys
High in Brooklyn, a post occupied only a few short years
earlier by Norman Mailer, end up building missiles, even
while going to peace marches on weekends? How did he
go from shyly slipping a napkin with the words MARRY ME
across a table at Peter Luger in Brooklyn to fathering four
unplanned and unexpected babies in six years?

An only child of Russian immigrants, my father was
shy and uncomfortable, at least when you first met him.
He was not a man the world embraced, with the exception of one very unusual day in 1947 when he was riding
the bus home from New York Polytechnic to the Canarsie
house where he still lived with his parents, Hymie and

Pauline. This day, to his surprise and confusion, when he reached his stop the African American passengers all began shouting and hugging one another, and then my dad. Jackie Robinson had just hit his first major-league home run.

If my dad wondered how he got here, I always wondered, why'd he stay? At the end of the dining-room table, the day's newspaper or the latest *New Yorker* in front of him, he did his best to ignore us all. A photo like this one, where he's helping out, or trying to, is at odds with my memories of him keeping his distance, sullen, or on the attack and yelling. It wasn't that he'd never tried to help. My mom jumped at every opportunity to tell the story of the time no one could figure out why my baby brother wouldn't stop crying, and she discovered it was because my dad had pinned my brother to the diaper. The story was one of many my mom drilled into us as part of her long and successful campaign to turn all of us kids against our dad.

The fate of my parents' marriage was sealed the day my father threw his in-laws out of their apartment in Flushing, Queens. My grandmother was dangling her car keys in front of my eight-month-old face when my dad decided he'd had enough, not just of this visit, but of all the intrusions of two people who'd never liked him from day one. So he simply told them to get out. When they were gone he said to my mother, "It's them or me." For the rest of my childhood, my grandparents visited only after we'd come home from school, always leaving before my dad got home from work. We'd meet for hours in the kinds of restaurants with big salad bars, trays, and endless refills of soda. When we got home, my dad would be waiting, but we were never allowed to tell him where we'd been. When I was in high school, my grandparents moved to a house about three miles from ours. This, too, we had to keep secret from my dad. Sometimes we'd pass him in the car as he drove home from work. He was always scowling.

Occasionally, though, a wonderful, anarchic sense of humor would emerge from under the layers of grumpy. One particularly chaotic evening, my dad pushed his blue vinyl-covered chair back from the table, and took his paper napkin off his lap. He unfolded it, tipped his head back, and carefully laid it over his face like a flag of surrender. We all froze and stared. Then he wiggled his tongue till it pushed through the thin white paper and out into the air.

Once my youngest brother graduated high school there was no longer any point in "staying together for the kids" and so, after twenty-one years, my mom filed for divorce and my dad left. To all our surprise, he embraced his second bachelorhood. He put a personal ad in *The New York Review of Books* under the headline: LIBERAL. LITERATE. LIBERATED. He actually dated. And most remarkable, he was able to look after himself. He was particularly proud of figuring out how to scramble eggs in a microwave. He seemed so content that I couldn't help but ask him why he had stayed married, despite seeming so miserable. "I didn't think I could take care of myself. I never had my own apartment. I didn't know how to cook or do laundry." I was speechless. "If I'd known how easy it was, I might have left sooner."

My mom remained invested in all of us hating our dad as much as she did, but over time my brothers and sister and I each came to embrace the heretical notion that he was not so bad. We went to art films with him, after which he'd try to pass Pauline Kael's opinion off as his own, but he never got mad at me for calling him on it. His intellectual pretensions did get on my nerves occasionally, particularly his propensity for mangling names. One afternoon as we were walking around the Guggenheim I lost my patience. "Dad! It's Bauhaus! Not Brauhaus! You're making me think of sausage." He looked genuinely hurt. "Why are you picking on me?" he asked.

This sounds like something a kid might say, but now I wonder if it was just my dad being sensitive, or an early step on his last, and most awful adventure. It was only five years between the time we realized something was very wrong with my father and his death from Alzheimer's, but his absentmindedness and inattention to detail went back years. How else could we have deceived him so easily?

As his mind's ability to deal with his present reality declined, more and more of the warmth and humor that had been buried resurfaced. Affectionate, funny, uninhibited, it was almost like he was reborn. My dad happily married a woman he had known his entire life, a third cousin actually, known for being very outgoing and a drinker. One day he became delusional and tried to hurt her, and she insisted he stay with my brother for a few days. When it was time for him to return home, he kept insisting to my brother that he was home already. My brother tried to convince him he was married and living in Manhattan, but my dad wasn't having any of it. When my brother told my dad the name of the woman he was married to, he snickered, remembering the loudmouthed girl he'd known for decades as a friend. My brother pointed to my dad's hand. When he looked down and saw the wedding ring on his finger, without missing a beat he blurted out, "Oh my God what have I gotten myself into?" It was the question he'd been asking himself all his life.

Philip Glist was born in New York City and raised in Bedford, Massachusetts. He currently lives in Venice, California, with his wife, Michelle Nordon, and son, Blue. He works as a creative director at Team One, an ad agency.

His essay was chosen after being submitted in a contest on the website.

patricia and jerry

by Mandy Stadtmiller

I THINK ABOUT MY PARENTS ALL THE TIME. Every day. Every second. There's almost nothing I do where I don't think about my parents. They are ridiculously outside the mainstream and absolutely badass.

My dad is blind. My mom is the chick who married a blind guy.

In 1968 my dad was a combat marine in Vietnam for one month. Then he took two AK-47 rounds in the face and was the only one to survive a sniper attack that left three other men from his squad dead.

To answer your question: Yes. My mom met him *after* he was shot.

That's the first thing everyone always asks. If that doesn't tell you about the world I don't know what does.

"Did they meet after he was shot or *before*?"

People want to know how other people measure up—if loyalty exists, what kind of a person my mom is . . . Steal a little window into her private psyche. It's such a great question, isn't it? Because it's socially acceptable versus all the other questions they want to ask.

Like: What's your mom's story anyway? Is she a saint who stuck by her man even after his face got blown apart?

No?

So then . . . what's her deal? What's wrong with her? Did she not think she could do better than a blind guy? And a blind, kind of fucked-up-looking guy who's had more than 150 surgeries to make him look less fucked-up?

Well, here's what kind of a person Patricia Stadtmiller is.

My mom was actually engaged to a very normal, very not-having-been-shot-twice-in-the-face man from her home state of Washington when she met my dad in that hippie-loving state of California.

Compared with the average dude—let's be honest—my dad was appalling.

Fresh from his injury, right when he was in the hospital, people would pass out when they came to visit him.

His face was an aggressive act. Like a visual fuck you.

You can't look away or deny what happened to him. Makes people fidget. What do you do with that? War? Well here you go. Meet Jerry Stadtmiller.

But it's true. His personality was and is an undeniable force of nature.

Charming, charismatic, funny, balls-out, joie de vivre in spades, the essence of what it means to understand the gratitude of life rather than slinking into depression, misery, and self-pity. The thing about my dad is, he made my mom feel better. She was depressed. He made her laugh. Yes, him. The dude shot twice in the face with the eye socket sewn over and the thing and all the other things.

My mom is this unforgettable, bizarre, incredibly clever, deathly shy, free-associative genius who's always been attracted to personalities who say what you're not supposed to say. My dad was the guy who would stand up to her domineering father and her what-would-the-Joneses-think mother. So, because people are all the same in terms of getting moony over and eventually marrying their parental archetype, she fell hard for my dad. She fell in love with his anger. And boy was he angry.

My dad's serious girlfriend of two years left him after he came back from the war just about as messed up as a human being can be. She simply couldn't handle it. My dad's rejection and abandonment from her and the rest of his family was thorough and complete. His mother had died two days before he was scheduled to leave for Vietnam and his brash, distant, man-about-town father was newly remarried to a second wife my dad didn't fully trust, didn't fully understand.

But my dad did not crumple. Did not quit. Never backed down. Neither of my parents ever did.

On August 8, 1970, my mom went against her parents' will, essentially choosing to be with the poster child for enraging the Joneses. They wed in La Jolla, California, on a wind-whipped little cove with cream cotton placards from that hippie song, "Come on people now, smile on your brother, everybody get together."

Two years later, my dad, still just a baby himself at the age of twenty-five, and my mom, five and a half years older at thirty, got pregnant with my sister. This is a picture of them then, mid-kiss, in the backyard of the house I grew up in on 60th Street in San Diego, overgrown with ivy and honeysuckle and care. Together, they are so happy, so in love, so positioned: the Stadtmillers against the world.

God how I love this photo.

God how I love my parents.

Here's why I think about them, every second of every day—the secret that keeps me going, always:

When I am scared, when people are telling me that I suck, when the Internet is saying I am an asshole, when I am telling myself I *am* an asshole, I just remember: the power of being who you know you have to be.

Because you absolutely have to be honest when you grow up with the parents that I did.

Everything else would be spiritual suicide, a denial of what is staring at you in the face as the world gawks from the sidelines.

See, the dirty little secret about me is: I try. Very, very hard. And I don't apologize for it. Sometimes people are unnerved by this. Especially cool people and hipsters and cool hipster people with all the right snide. Because nothing makes people fidget like ambition and earnest individuals. Where's the joke? Where's the detachment? Where's the irony? Where's the hatred? Are you risking? *Oh my God, she's trying. She's actually trying.*

And I'm all for coolness and hip. Totally great at parties and for jokes. But I think even more powerful is the truth of being who you were born to be.

Who I am is the daughter of Jerry and Pat Stadtmiller.

And I don't give a damn what other people think of me.

Especially those assholes the Joneses.

Mandy Stadtmiller hopes you get what you want out of life. You can read her at MandyStadtmiller.com.

deborah

by Katherine Center

ONE DAY, WHEN MY MOTHER WAS six, she decided to take a horseback ride by herself.

This was Texas in the late '40s, and there were horses aplenty—especially at her wildcatter uncle's ranch. My mom and her cousins used to roam the vast territory of Pecan Acres every weekend while their parents kept a loose eye on them from the screen porch. Kids ran free back then in ways we can't even imagine now, and even in the city, they'd scamper the neighborhood with their dogs all summer—only called in for lunch and supper.

But at the ranch, there were horses.

The kids played hide-and-seek on them, and rode into town for ice cream, and explored. My mom had an older brother and a passel of boy cousins, and she was always trying to keep up.

As a teenager, my mom would learn to square dance on horseback at a full gallop. She'd ride bareback against the rules into the deepest parts of the Guadalupe River to let her horse swim, floating above its back in the water. In college at Smith, she would try riding English and practice jumping all winter in the barn. Many years later, after her children were grown, she would get thrown and break her ribs while galloping full-tilt across the wilds of Montana. Even as a grandma, she spends a week every year riding—now more slowly—with friends.

But that would all come later: That would come after she'd learned how to read a horse the way any good rider must, and after she'd internalized the confidence it takes to sit on the shoulders of a thousand-pound animal and tell it what to do, and after years of exploring and investigating and learning to trust her instincts seeped into her sense of who she was. Here is the truth: She didn't become a cowgirl after a lifetime on horseback; she spent a lifetime on horseback because early on she had already become a cowgirl.

I rode horseback when I was a girl, too—a bit, at summer camp. At the same summer camp, actually, where my mother had been an Aztec Chief and worn an enormous green headdress. I had her same riding instructor—a horsewoman who continued to ride past age one hundred and now has a spot in the Cowgirl Hall of Fame—but I was a disappointment. I could stay on a horse, but I couldn't ride.

My mom could ride, and she still can. Even years of office work and high heels, city living, and carpool driving didn't take it from her. She knows how to ride the way she knows how to breathe.

She credits weekends at her uncle's ranch from infancy. Her mother was an identical twin who spent as much time as possible with her sister, which meant the whole gang was out in the country all the time.

The best horse there was Peter Pan. He was a retired circus horse, so smooth the kids could ride him standing up—bareback and barefoot. They could crawl beneath his belly and between his legs with-out spooking him. They could hang from his neck. He was a big old paint with room for four, or five, or even six kids on his back at once. And he never seemed to mind.

And this is how independent those kids were: My mom's uncle placed concrete steps by the hitching post for them to mount the horses—so they could get up and ride whenever they liked, once they were old enough.

I took my daughter riding last summer, when she was six. She loved every minute of it, but I can't help but contrast the helmet and fancy boots she wore, the riding instructor with a lead rope moni-toring every step, and the nervous mother—me—with a Flip video recording every memorable second. At that same age, my mom was racing the boys back to the barn.

This is what I see in my mind when my mom tells me about the day that, as a six-year-old, she took off riding by herself:

My scrappy little redheaded mother stands in the yard alone. The big boys have ridden off without her, again. She eyes Peter Pan at the hitching post, unties him, and climbs the mounting block to get on. No hesitation. Just that same matter-of-fact competence that still defines her to this day. She guides her horse onto the gravel lane with just a nudge of her heels to his belly. She's got the reins in her hands and rests her fingers on his black mane. Maybe she's off to find the boys, or maybe she's just exploring—but soon she's cantering along, leaning into Peter Pan's withers, as sure-footed as the horse himself as they gallop off toward the pecan grove.

She's probably wearing jeans, and boots, and a plaid western shirt with pearl snaps and maybe some ruffles. It's almost impossible to imagine your parents as children—as anything other than the adults who raised you—but now that I have a daughter who looks almost exactly like my mother did at that age, it's easier. Same big blue eyes and fair skin. Same freckles. Same long legs. And my mom was probably missing some front teeth at that age, now that I think about it, the way my little one is missing her teeth right now.

And there's my six-year-old mother, riding off on her own without permission, not yet aware that there's a low branch directly in her path—one she won't notice until it's too late, or won't be able to avoid. One that'll knock her right off the horse and knock her out.

They'll find her a little later, not too far out, waking up in the grass, Peter Pan standing patiently beside her and a bruise on her forehead. It's the first of many injuries she'll get from riding. And, of course, from life. And it's a moment when her young self might have brushed shoulders with the adult she'd grow up to be: a woman who has never thought twice about bravery. Because she doesn't know any other way to ride.

✳ ✳ ✳

Katherine Center is the author of three comic novels about love and family— *The Bright Side of Disaster, Everyone Is Beautiful,* and *Get Lucky*—and has another on the way in 2012. Her books and essays have appeared in *Redbook, People, USA Today, Vanity Fair, Real Simple, The Dallas Morning News,* and the *Houston Chronicle,* as well as the anthology *Because I Love Her: 34 Women Writers on the Mother–Daughter Bond.* She lives in her hometown of Houston, Texas, with her husband and two young children—and tries every day to be as awesome as her mom.

carol and jimmy

by Laurie Notaro

"HANG ON," MY DAD SAID, holding out the phone in midair. I could tell because of the fuzzy, static silence that surrounded it, and the faraway volume of his voice as he yelled to the downstairs, "CA-ROL! Laurie's on the phone. She wants to know when you are going to be lonesome!"

"*Awesome,* Dad," I yelled into the phone. "I said *awesome.*"

A few more silent seconds passed before I heard an assortment of muffled sounds.

"Yeah," my father said into the receiver. "She's pretending not to hear me. She hears me. I know her game."

I sighed. "Tell her that I'm QVC and that there's something wrong with one of her orders," I told my dad, who loudly relayed the lie.

"Hello?" she said so quickly I never heard her pick up the line. "What's wrong? Which order? Is it the Rachael Ray FoodTastic 4-in-1 Thermal Carrier with Baker Taker or the Paula Deen's Smithfield 3.5 Pound Smoked and Sliced Beef Brisket with the Three-Tiered Meat Caddy? Which one is it? Is there a problem with this month's delivery of Paula Deen's Boneless Breasts? Because when you tell me her boneless breasts will be sitting on my front porch every four weeks, I expect it every four weeks, just like a breast magazine!"

"It's me, Mom," I confessed.

"You didn't tell me that the Paula Deen breasts had been sitting out on the porch in the sun," my father interrupted. "Don't feed me that again. I know your game."

"I'm not lonesome," my mother shot back. "Stop calling me about it."

"It's *awesome*," I corrected her. "It's about when you were *awesome*. I want you to tell me some funny stories from the time when you were dating."

Neither one of them said anything, though I heard them both breathing and I heard my mother change the channel.

The silence was becoming uncomfortable as my parents both breathed into the phone, one upstairs, one downstairs.

Finally, it was my mother who broke it. "Are you going to get in trouble if you don't do this?" she asked. "We don't have any funny stories. I don't know what you want me to do. Make something up."

"Everyone has funny stories," I insisted. "Try to think. You have to have at least one before you were married."

Silence again. One second. Two seconds. Three. Four. Five.

My mother put an end to the torture. "I told you, nothing funny ever hap—"

"Hey, I've got a story!" my father blurted suddenly, and then started to laugh. "This is before we were married. This is a good one.

It's good. We went on a picnic with Nana and Pop Pop, and your mother and I had waded a little bit into the lake, but we were just standing there in the part that had been roped off for little kids because it was really cold. All of a sudden, Pop Pop came charging down to the lake, yelling, 'Whaddya doing standing there! Come on, go in!' and he dove into the lake, and starting swimming. We could see him swimming under the water, and he was heading straight for a wooden pole that had the rope tied to it. All of a sudden, we saw the pole shake, and a couple of seconds later, Pop Pop stood up, holding his head."

"Okay, there's your funny story," my mother confirmed. "Can I hang up now? *Ace of Cakes* is on and he's making a giant BLT. I need to see this. He's making cake lettuce. It's important."

"Well, I think it's a great story, but it doesn't really count as a dating story," I tried to explain. "I need a story that happened to you guys. Think back to when you were teenagers. You both went to New Utrecht High School."

"That's the school they based *Welcome Back, Kotter* on," my father bragged. "It was a crazy school!"

"Yeah," my mother agreed. "It was a crazy school."

"Great!" I said, getting excited. "Tell me about that!"

"Oh, well," my mother said. "Nothing really happened."

"Yeah, nothing really happened," my father agreed.

I decided to try a different approach. "You guys grew up in Brooklyn, a five-minute ride to the greatest city on earth," I reminded them. "You had to have done some exciting things in Manhattan, right?"

"Oh, sure," my father offered. "I used to work in the Flatiron Building. My first day was exciting. After that, not really."

"I've never been to the Empire State Building or the Statue of Liberty," my mother scoffed. "So what. Big deal. I've seen plenty of buildings. Going into a building makes you exciting? Since when? I don't need to walk into a big fancy building. I went to New Utrecht High School."

"But you said nothing happened there," I responded.

"Nothing did," she said again. "Oh, wait! Wait! I have a story about New York! Oh, this is good. Okay, so Daddy and I and Nana and Pop Pop went out to dinner to some very fancy restaurant in the city. I don't remember what I ordered. Do you remember what I ordered, Jimmy?"

"No," my father said blankly.

"Anyway," my mother continued. "When we were ready to leave, Nana got her black lamb fur coat, and we left. We were almost to the car when we noticed that her sleeves were way too long. We couldn't even see her hands! She looked like Dopey! She had taken the wrong coat, because everyone, you know, had Persian lamb coats then. It wasn't even her coat!"

"That's another great story," I admitted. "But it didn't happen to you. I need a story that happened to you."

"That's ridiculous," my mother protested. "I was there."

"Okay . . . ," I said, my mind searching. "How did Dad propose, then?"

"I didn't," he said quickly.

"He didn't," my mother confirmed. I had already done the math when I was in seventh grade with the rest of my biology class. I was the firstborn, arriving two years after they had been married. No funny story there.

"Oh, I know!" my mother suddenly said. "There was this time that all of Dad's family went to Grandma's for a party and we all stayed the night, the girls in one room and the boys in the other. Then, in the girls' room, Aunt Rose got a sheet and did a striptease behind it, and were we laughing! It was hysterical. I laughed so hard I cried."

"That's great," I agreed. "But that was someone else, too. I need a story about *you.*"

"Maybe you're getting a little too friggin' picky about your stories," she shot back. "Maybe that's the problem here."

"What about your honeymoon?" I scrambled. "That has to be exciting. Right? You went to Florida. Didn't you have fun then?"

"No," my dad said before I was even finished.

"I got sunburned the first day we were there," my mother related. "And we were there for another friggin' week in the sun. We could only go to dark places. Like the movies. Or the aquarium."

"But mostly the room," my father added. "With the shades drawn."

"I had second-degree burns," my mother went on. "Everything hurt. Especially being touched. Very painful. I looked like the bacon that Ace is making the frosting out of. I'm missing it while I'm playing games with you, and that is almost half the sandwich."

"It's a quarter, Carol. Bread, bacon, lettuce, tomato. A quarter. All right," my dad said with a deep breath. "I gotta go back to work. Did you get what you need?"

"Actually not real—" I began when I heard the line upstairs click, and it was just me and my mom.

"So good luck with your story," my mother said after a sigh.

"Yeah, thanks," I replied, wondering how I was going to pull this thing off.

"Use the Pop Pop story," she advised. "Everyone always laughs at that."

"I think I'm going to make stuff up," I concluded aloud.

"Oh. Look. That's a rolling pin. He's making the lettuce," my mother alerted me. "I'm hanging up."

"Awesome," I replied.

✳ ✳ ✳

Laurie Notaro has seen ghosts twice in her life: once on her tenth birthday and again when she mistakenly assumed her husband had come home at 2 AM dressed as Dashiell Hammett. Notaro hasn't made her bed in thirty-two years, was said by *The New Yorker* to have "positively cackled" (a gross exaggeration), and is the author of eight books, including *The Idiot Girls' Action-Adventure Club, The Autobiography of a Fat Bride,* and her most recent novel, *Spooky Little Girl*. She still lives in Eugene, Oregon, with her opaque husband and absurdly charming dog, Maeby.

heather and ian

by Gabrielle Nancarrow

MY MUM AND DAD KISSED BEFORE they spoke. On a ship sailing from Melbourne, Australia, to London in 1972, a beautiful twenty-year-old in a red dress casually strolled up to a skinny guy bathed in tattoos and tight jeans and kissed him. "Pretend you're with me," she said as she jumped into his arms (seriously). He caught her and kissed her back, just as the girl he had been dating for two weeks walked out of the bathroom. In a moment, Mum had met the man she would spend the rest of her life with. She had also successfully freed herself from the adoring guy who had been pursuing her for a week and who saw her jump into a stranger's arms. Dad's date turned and walked away.

I have imagined this scene so many times, the night my

parents met. I wish I had a photo of it just to see them in that moment. But it's also nice to simply imagine: the red dress, the cute guy, the very spontaneous embrace that successfully ended their respective flings and marked the beginning of their lives together.

Mum and Dad were sailing on the *Fairstar*, which made regular trips to London in the '60s and '70s carrying a boatload of carefree young Aussies looking for good times in the motherland. Mum had dreamed of living in London since she was six years old and had been saving her whole life for this adventure. Dad jumped on at the last minute with less than a hundred pounds to his name.

Six weeks into their journey, the *Fairstar* docked for a night in Cape Town, South Africa. Dad made a quick decision to end his voyage there to go surfing with mates, despite the fact that the love of his life was on board and he was out of cash. This was a pretty typical move for Dad; crazy maybe, but also impulsive, bold. He was absolutely living for the moment then, as he does now. Time and age have not dampened his intrepid spirit, and to this day he still embodies the best parts of his teenage self: his strength, humor, optimism, and relaxed nature.

And Mum didn't seem to mind, either. She simply waved him good-bye, claims she forgot about him, and continued on her journey to London. I don't know how long it took Dad to work out that he might have let a good one go but it can't have been too long before he called his parents, asked them for a loan, and bought a ticket on a flight to London, because he was there in the crowd waiting for Mum when the *Fairstar* docked two weeks later. I doubt he knew it at the time but I believe it was in this very decision that Dad began to let go of his rebellious youth and start on a journey toward something much deeper than his tattoos and tough exterior.

Mum, however, was quite surprised to see Dad there on the dock waiting for her. Fiercely independent and seeking the life of a single girl in '70s London, she certainly hadn't come to find a man and settle down. So she left with her brother from the dock that day and told Dad she would "see him around."

So they started their lives in London, continuing the well-worn path of so many Australians before them, living in the north and working at the pub. Mum was living her dream and Dad was just happy to be experiencing a new city, a new life. These were pretty carefree times and there seemed to be no pressure to go to college and pursue a career. They saw each other around and were soon planning adventures together: touring in a combie van through the European summer, visiting Israel, Egypt, Morocco, Russia. They grew closer. They fell in love. Their experiences were richer than most people are lucky to have in a lifetime.

This photo was taken in Paris four years after they met, in 1976. Mum was twenty-four, Dad twenty-six. Exactly three months before this shot was taken, Dad asked Mum to marry him in a small hotel room in Venice (they couldn't afford a gondola ride). Dad had just beaten Mum at a game of cards. She was mad and threw the cards at him. His reaction? "Marry me." Mum didn't say yes. But she didn't say no, either. She said she would think about it and flew home to Australia for three months. Mum never did say yes, but she did agree to fly back to Europe to be with Dad again. They settled in Malta. One weekend they went to Paris and posed for this photo in front of Notre Dame. Mum was wearing a pink top. Dad had moved from skinny jeans to double denim.

Two years later, on December 2, 1978, they married in a small church on a hill just down the road from where Mum grew up in county Victoria, Australia. A minister named John Lamont married them. When I got married in February 2009, I searched everywhere for that minister who married my parents thirty years before. I wanted this man to marry us too. My mum and dad have had such a beautiful and adventurous life together and I felt that if I tracked this man down and he too married us, our life together would be as happy as theirs has been. Mum helped me find him and so far, so good.

Mum and Dad settled in Anglesea, a small coastal town on the spectacular Great Ocean Road. And, as it was in the beginning, they traveled, now with four children in tow. I am their second child, their eldest daughter. I have an older brother Ben, twenty-nine, and two younger sisters, Justine, twenty-three and Monique, nineteen. For as long as I have known, Dad has worked overseas. He would work for a month, and then come home for a month, and sometimes we would meet him at the end of his time away for a family holiday—in Thailand, Paris, Peru, Hong Kong, Italy, the United States. We have traveled the world together. As great as this was, it wasn't always easy for us, and especially for Mum, with Dad away for half our lives. But Mum is the most incredible woman I will ever know. It is because of her that we are each other's best friends. She is strong and absolutely selfless. Above all, Mum loves us with a fierce passion. When I am with her, everything is okay. If I am even half the mum she is one day, I will have achieved something wonderful.

Today Mum and Dad, Heather and Ian, live in Rio de Janeiro, Brazil. They moved there two years ago when Dad's job was transferred from Lagos in Nigeria to Rio. For the first time in their married life, Dad comes home from work at the end of the day. For the first time in her life, Mum can see and understand what Dad does for a living. I believe they bring out the best in each other, and in us, that their friendship and hard work has kept them together, and that their love makes life complete.

My dad's first girlfriend was named Pamela Arrowsmith. He once bought her a can of hair spray. Mum was proposed to twice before she met Dad. I'm just glad they found each other, and that the girl in the red dress was confident enough to walk up to a cute guy in tight jeans and kiss him.

✳ ✳ ✳

Gabrielle Nancarrow loves to write, travel, and take photos. In her twenty-seven years she has visited more than a hundred cities in twenty-five countries and has lived in Melbourne, Paris, New York, and Buenos Aires.

Her essay was chosen after being submitted in a contest on the website.

phil and karen

by Mollie Glick

MY PARENTS WERE INTRODUCED BY A DOG. It was 1974 and
my mom was an honors student at the University of
Pennsylvania. As far as I can tell, her previous suitors included a cape-wearing poet and an introverted doctoral
student who horrified my grandparents by reading *The
New York Times* at the breakfast table when he came to
visit. Hers was a nerdy crew, so she wasn't exactly making
eyes at the blond-haired, blue-eyed, muttonchopped captain of the track team. But he'd noticed her. And he'd noticed the red plaid deerstalker cap into which she'd tucked
her curly black hair when she walked her dog around
campus.

The dog's name was Toto. He was a classic "whodunit"
mutt with the large pricked ears of a German shepherd

and the short-legged body of a corgi. One of her friends, a veterinary student, had found him on the street and suggested my mom take him in. He was absolutely devoted to her, but after living on the streets for so long, he had a propensity to stray. In fact, he was so intelligent that he usually found his own way back to her dorm, and could even be seen riding the elevator up to her floor.

But this time, Toto didn't need to retrace his own steps, because my father spotted him trotting around campus on his short little legs, and immediately recognized him as my mom's dog. This was the opening he'd been waiting for. He used his track-and-field skills to catch the stray pup, and carried him all the way back to my mom's dorm wrapped in his beige corduroy field coat.

✳ ✳ ✳

Mollie Glick is a literary agent and freelance writer whose work has been published in *W* magazine, *Fugue,* and *Writer's Digest*. She recently adopted a mutt of her own.

marty and aveva

by Rachel Shukert

BEFORE I WAS BORN, my parents did a lot of things that sound interesting or, dare I say, awesome.

On their first date in 1971, they went to a performance of nonlinear experimental theater, an art form neither of them has willingly witnessed since.

They spent their honeymoon in 1973 backpacking around Europe, struggling with the rapidly plummeting dollar and developing an unyielding enmity toward the nation and people of France.

They lived in Berkeley, California, just a few blocks away from where Patty Hearst was held by the Symbionese Liberation Army. ("I never saw her," my mother said. "It wasn't like I was going to run into her at the grocery store.")

They shrugged off the Shukerts' fifty-year legacy of professional butchery (of animals, that is; the Shukerts only "break down" in the figurative sense) and turned to lifelong vegetarianism, which may or may not qualify as "awesome," depending on your point of view, but was certainly a singularly elegant act of youthful rebellion.

My mother worked as a bookkeeper for the United Artists film company, and was present for the making of *Chitty Chitty Bang Bang.* My father watched two episodes of the original *Star Trek* every afternoon for a full year, and futzed around making stained-glass hanging lamps and playing his guitar with the *all you need is love* sticker on the case.

They moved to Austin and had furniture made out of orange crates and burlap, just like hobos. They also saw a lot of early Kinky Friedman shows.

Then they moved back to Omaha, where they were from. My father began a meteoric rise through the halls of city government (although due to his particular brand of vague social anxiety and unimpeachable integrity, never ran for elected office). My mother passed the Nebraska psychologists' licensing exam, began her clinical practice, and was delivered of the bald, wriggling bundle of tiresome neurosis and pointless insecurity that would eventually devolve into yours truly.

Some might say that this was the end of the era of my parents' relative awesomeness, but I don't think they would be among this proverbial "some." Because once I was belched into the world, they were at last able to channel their formidable creative and iconoclastic energies to a single greater purpose: scaring the shit out of me.

Let me tell you about this game we used to play when I was about two or three, before my sister was born and somehow made my parents normal.

My father would have me sit on one of the maroon velvet love seats in our living room, and tell me if I sat still like a good girl, I would get a wonderful surprise.

Toddling fool that I was, I trusted him.

My father would leave the room for a moment, and return composed and impersonal, like a conductor about to lift his baton. He sat at the piano, his hands poised for a deliberative moment over the keys before he brought them crashing down into the first, ominous chords of "Also Sprach Zarathustra" by Richard Strauss. I felt a shiver of anticipation creep down my tiny spine. He played on, louder and louder, until the music lamp on the top of the piano buzzed dangerously with the vibration. Another chord, another, until suddenly, at the deafening climax, my mother burst from out of the broom closet underneath the stairs and came charging toward me, her round green eyes bulging out of her head, hooting and flailing like a crazed chimpanzee.

I screamed in terror and tried to flee up the stairs. But my legs were short and my mother the ape blocked my way, her yowls and shrieks drowning out even my father's relentless keyboard.

She would not break character until I began to sob in earnest, and they both fell about laughing like maniacs.

"It's the 'Dawn of Man' from *2001: A Space Odyssey,*" my father gasped, wiping his eyes with his callused thumb.

My mother guffawed: "You should see the look on your face!"

It's taken twenty-five years, but I think I've finally come up with the comeback to this my limited language skills at the time would not allow: "And you should see what you've just made me do to my big-girl pants."

While this scenario is the only one I can remember of them colluding in their terrorizing of me, it was far from the only one. My father liked slowly looming into unsuspecting people's field of vision while wearing a full-face rubber Albert Einstein mask that looked at once real and horrifyingly unreal, like when Hannibal Lecter put that guy's face over his face, and once a soft spot or irrational phobia was revealed, he was merciless in needling. As a small child, I was frightened of the life-sized model elephants in the entry hall of the natural history museum. The elephants stood reared on their back legs with their tusks menacingly in the air, while an ambient sound-track of angry trunk blasts played in the background. For much longer than I care to admit, I would beg my mother to reassure me that "the elephants were in their house." She would oblige, and I would be placated—that is, until my father sidled up beside me and whispered "No, they're not."

My mother, who had proved her considerable acting chops with the bone-wielding ape bit, preferred to disappear into characters when she wanted to disturb. You'd be sitting at the kitchen table, having a perfectly normal afternoon snack, when suddenly her eyes would glaze over and in a faraway voice she would say: "Why are you calling me 'Mommy'? I'm not your mommy. I'm a time traveler from another dimension," and no amount of pleading, or even tears, could get her to recant until she was good and ready. But at least the Time Traveler was essentially benign: She may not be "Mommy" but at least she didn't wish you any physical harm. The same could not be said for the entity known as "Monster Doll," a Mengele/Chucky hybrid with a penchant for describing the various bloodcurdling medical experiments she was plotting, the insinuation being that they would somehow turn *you* into a monstrous plaything like her. Maybe that doesn't sound scary to you, but it wasn't your mother. I'm almost thirty years old and I'm still scared of Monster Doll.

Over the years, I've wondered what was behind this seeming need of my parents to frighten me. Were they acting out scenarios of their own ambivalence, or even latent resentment about being a parent? Were they frightening me so they could reassure me, or allowing me to face my own fears in order to overcome them, *Uses of Enchantment*–style? Or maybe, only a generation removed from the horrors of Europe, they were trying to induct me into a cruel and unpredictable world: a world in which a loving mother could transform irrevocably into an aloof dimension-hopping alien was one in which a friendly neighbor could become an oppressor, a murderer. After a string of such hypotheses, my therapist finally suggested something novel: that I just ask them.

"I don't know," said my mother. She giggled. "I guess we just thought it was really damn funny."

Which, even I have to admit, is a little bit awesome.

✳ ✳ ✳

Rachel Shukert is the author of *Everything Is Going to Be Great* and *Have You No Shame? and Other Regrettable Stories.* Her work has been featured on NPR and in *Salon, Slate, McSweeney's,* and *The Daily Beast,* among others. She lives in New York City.

azra and ilarion

by Veronica Lara

IT MADE NO SENSE. HOW COULD she leave her family for a man she could hardly understand? How could he feed her when he could hardly feed himself? How would her devoutly Muslim parents react to the news that they'd fallen in love? How can a Pakistani woman and Bolivian man raise a family?

From a distance these questions sound puzzling, but faith can do wonders—and at ages twenty-one and twenty-three it seemed perfectly logical.

Azra Ali Khan was originally named Sofia, but her parents changed her name as part of a custom after she fell ill as a baby. She was born in Karachi, Pakistan, and lived a quiet life in the equivalent of a massive mansion—but she would never have called herself wealthy. Her father and mother were Musharraf and Aftab, a diplomat and homemaker. Musharraf had enduring memories of the violence during the 1947 India–Pakistan partition, but he made a comfortable life for his family. As part of his profession Musharraf had the great fortune of granting his family travel to the United States—with visas fully covered. Once in New York, Azra and her four siblings could have education arranged for them, too. More important, her parents began preparing a match for her. This was tradition and this was how Musharraf and Aftab themselves got married; after all, parents knew their children's needs the best. Although Azra's wedding would be a joyous affair, she would need to conceal her happiness out of modesty—much like a bride who "blushes." This was all custom, and, like a minuet, everyone knew their positions and no one questioned what could happen if but one person fell out of step.

Ilarion Guillermo Lara Arcienega came to the United States at age seventeen from La Paz to study, plant his roots, and thrive. For some time he was in the country illegally, cleaning dishes and busing tables so he could earn enough to enroll himself in community college. He would have liked to have girlfriends, but they were expensive and with the little free time he had from working various jobs he preferred to sleep. Living in a nice lady's basement, he owned only a makeshift bed and a few personal belongings he could easily part with in case he had to flee from the INS. In Bolivia only the sons of the richest families could afford a US college education, certainly not folks like Ilarion who had worked since the age of five and was grateful that for the first time in his life he had running water. His parents were Jose and Maria, a nurse and engineer who worked tirelessly to ensure he had primary and secondary education—a rarity among his peers. They spoke Quechua, the Incan tongue, but for some reason they never passed down this tradition to his generation. Carrying their hopes intermixed with his determination, he was in New York and hungry for everything.

Although neither Azra or Ilarion spoke much English, they ended up meeting each other in a communications class at LaGuardia Community College. Ilarion would sing Azra Beatles songs while playing on his small *charango,* a Bolivian classical guitar, and Azra would just laugh. She was not accustomed to romance, but small gestures of love translate universally. She could tell he had a good heart and would eventually do anything possible to support his family; this was much more appealing than a man who merely inherited wealth. It was a risk, but she allowed the true tenets of her faith to guide her and see past his class, race, culture, language, and religion, and accepted a life of immediate poverty. At the time her family did not approve of her decision, yet although she had lived a sheltered life she felt secure in her judgment. Her shiny black hair and large expressive eyes made him notice her, but he was ultimately charmed by her ability to see *him,* unlike the customers at restaurants he worked at and passengers on trains who treated him as if he were invisible. Years of living in fear, working for change and even once for food (at a restaurant in Miami that shall go unnamed), left him feeling very lonely. He knew he had a mission, but the loneliness at times attacked his morale.

Marrying her bolstered his will to work even harder. She had never focused much on education since her prewritten destiny was read to her at an early age: Once she married she would become a wife and mother foremost. But being with him and seeing his almost superhuman diligence inspired her to work harder herself and truly become his partner. When they had me in 1983 they were still in school and juggling jobs. At one point we all ate yogurt because it was the only thing we could afford. I would not have known the difference; as with any first-time parents every shiver was a catastrophe and crying for no reason sent their hearts racing. They decided it would be best for me to live in Bolivia for a few years with my father's parents until they could get their feet on firmer ground. I was gone, but by the time I returned they had already set up a lovely nest.

We are all still together and joined by three more siblings: Isaac, Amy, and Cristina. My parents may have come from different places, but their unconquerable values of strong family, hard work, and appreciation for whatever you have (whether it is a lot or a little) still resonate today. My father had an ambitious vision while my mother helped preserve our integrity as a family. Earlier in their lives, both of them could have instead moved to the skyrocketing economies of nearby India and Brazil; but like Musharraf and Aftab and Jose and Maria who came before them, they clutched to higher hopes.

✳ ✳ ✳

Veronica Lara covers emerging markets and investment risk for *The Economist*'s business intelligence unit, the EIU, in New York. She is engaged to marry the love of her life, Langston Payne, whom she met in college at the University of Pennsylvania. She holds a master's degree from New York University and in her spare time she enjoys writing on her website, Beauty Revolver.

Her essay was chosen after being submitted in a contest on the website.

david and maria

by Anita Serwacki

I WONDER WHAT A BOOKIE WOULD have set the spread at on my human existence. As the genetic brew of two human beings from opposite sides of the world with pretty much nothing in common, and who only met due to a freak series of events involving duplicity, Antarctica, and a touch of stalking, I figure a one-dollar bettor would have come away with a life's worth of going-around money.

My father, a well-known charmer and hell raiser, recused himself from the educational system in the eighth grade. At seventeen he decided to take flight from the tumultuous tavern his parents ran in Buffalo, New York's Polish neighborhood known as Kaisertown, to join the US Navy, aiming to get his equivalency, learn some skills, and see the world. He became part of the

SeaBees construction unit and was eventually stationed in Rota, Spain.

While there, he came across a notice offering a chance to join a support team for the scientific research facilities at McMurdo base in Antarctica. It looked like it could be a kick, so he filled out an application. A year passed and he still hadn't received a response. The Vietnam conflict was percolating, and as the days went on he became convinced he had a better chance of getting shipped off to Saigon than to the Ice. Then out of the blue, he received orders to report in D.C. to undergo pre-acceptance tests for the program.

While he passed the physical with flying colors, it was followed by the required psych tests, which for him were a little trickier. The navy needed to be sure its recruits for the project did not harbor antisocial dispositions, as they were to be part of a skeleton crew that would spend six months in isolated darkness during the raging South Pole winter. If the movie *The Thing* has taught us anything, it is that Antarctica can cause people to lose their shit (with or without the presence of space-alien-infected huskies). My father, who, let's say, came from a family that tilted to the antisocial side of the spectrum, was a little liberal with the truth. They asked him questions such as "Did your family have quarrels?" He said, "Every question, I knew what the dude was looking for, so I says 'Yeah, of course, me and my old man get along great!'" Somehow he psyched out the psychologists and made it into the final, elite pool out of the initial two thousand who had initially applied.

His trip to Antarctica began on a prop plane in Rhode Island with a brief layover in New Zealand. While he thought he was going to get a little Kiwi R&R before being carried onward to the end of the earth, instead he had two hours to be processed before being crammed like a sardine on a military plane for the final leg.

After a roughly twelve-hour flight, he finally arrived in Antarctica.

I don't think I can do proper justice to his initial reaction upon landing, so I'll just quote my father from a chat I taped with him a few
years ago. "I'm walking down the ramp, I breathe . . . temperature is
like twenty below zero. I can't get my breath! I gotta take my coat
and cover my face to get my breath. And I'm looking around and I
don't see *nothing* but miles and miles of nothing but ice. I says, *What
the fuck did I get myself into?* Then I get in the helicopter. I'm looking and there is nothing, but *nothing* over there. The helicopter goes
over the glaciers and I see a couple huts . . . it's the base. I says, you
mean I gotta fuckin' live here for a year? Fuck me. This is sick! Really
sick!"

My father was assigned to maintain the fuel systems for the entire
base. He was twenty-one years old.

After the one-year stint in Antarctica, my father put in for orders
for a stint in New Zealand. Several of my father's more gung-ho
navy-mates instead wanted to head directly out to 'Nam and tried to
get my father to join them. Screw that, he said. After a year in sub-
zero hell, he was damned if he was going to get shot at in a hundred-
degree jungle. Unfortunately, none of those friends who ventured to
Vietnam ended up making it back.

Beyond not being killed, it was a good choice on my father's part
because very soon he was to meet my mother in New Zealand. But
for them, it was not love at first sight.

A naïve, but lovely, whip-smart Catholic schoolgirl who grew up
on the grounds of a Christchurch park where her father was care-
taker, my mother graduated high school at fifteen and had already
spent several years working in Australia and New Zealand as a legal
secretary when my father rolled into town.

He and my mother met when she was casually dating his roommate. She initially couldn't stand my father. He had almost OCD
clean-freak tendencies and would grab a plate to wash it before a

person could even set it down. But my father had been harboring romantic intentions, so when the brief dalliance with the roommate fizzled, he made his move and badgered her to go out with him. She finally relented.

They went out to a nightclub and, to her surprise, had a nice time. He was a perfect non-OCD gentleman. However, after a few more dates over the course of the next week, things got a little weird. My father proposed marriage and started insisting she sign immigration papers to come to the States—immediately. She politely deferred, but he would not be deterred.

For some reason this did not adequately freak her out, and they continued to date. But now each night when he would drop her off, my father would just sleep in his car outside her house. He was there when she went to bed, there when she awoke. But instead of seeing him as some kind of stalker, she and her family took pity on him like a poor little stray puppy. At first, he was invited to stay the night on a couch in the kitchen. Then he was upgraded to the spare bedroom.

And after three months, my mother finally agreed to marry the dashing, yet peculiar, Yank navy man who was crashing down the hall.

Almost immediately following their picture-perfect reception at the historic Sign of the Takahe castle in Christchurch, he whisked her halfway around the world to a tarantula-infested military base on the Texas border, and then on to Kaisertown, New York, where people didn't take too kindly to book-reading foreign girls with weird accents who were not Polish.

But that's another chapter in the story . . .

Postscript: After forty-three years, and contrary to most predictions, my parents are, in fact, still married.

✳ ✳ ✳

Anita Serwacki is a contributing writer for *The Onion* and maintains the blog Meat Crimes (http://meatcrimes.tumblr.com). Previously she has written for the PBS cartoon *WordGirl,* and co-authored the books *The New Vampire's Handbook, The Devious Book for Cats,* and *The Dangerous Book for Dogs.* She lives in Brooklyn, New York.

wayne and margaret

by Hannah Brown Gordon

WHEN MY PARENTS TELL THE STORY OF how they met, surprisingly (or unsurprisingly, depending on if you know them) there are two very different versions of the story.

What they do agree upon is that they were at a social gathering at my father's apartment. They had met previously in 1969, in passing, but nothing had come of it. When they met again, the time it really counted, it was the fall of 1974 and New York City was falling apart around them. I mean, the city was literally broke. Certain areas reduced to a proverbial Wasteland.

My mother had recently moved to Manhattan from Kansas, where she had gone to school for her master's in psychology. But Kansas was the past with things that needed forgetting, so my mother got herself out of there and landed a job at the Rusk Institute for Rehabilitation

Medicine. Working with my father, as it happens. They remembered each other from 1969. They talked. They were colleagues. They liked each other. They may have even flirted (at work!).

My father, being the debonair guy he is, invited my mother over to his apartment with a few others they knew. Would she like to come over to his place for some food? She said yes. Eight o'clock? Yes, okay, yes she'd be there and bring a bottle of wine.

But other than those basic facts, they remember things very differently.

My mother says that my father had his eye set on her from the beginning. That she knew he was interested and so she followed his lead. He was by her side from the time she entered the apartment until she left. He sat next to her. He had the gaze in his eyes that men have, she says, when they're making their "intentions known." His apartment on the Upper West Side was rather small, so when he wanted to show her the "fantastic view of Central Park" from the other room? Yes, okay, she said, that sounds nice.

My father says that my mother flirted with him recklessly that night. She wore a low-cut dress, showing off her cleavage. She laughed, complimented him on his jokes (which can lean toward the corny, but it's very cute when he tells a joke because you can tell he's a little proud of himself—something I love, at least), and may have even touched his arm or knee a few times unnecessarily, leaned a bit too far forward, exposing even more of said cleavage. She may have even been wearing a push-up bra, he says.

He said, she said. You get it.

I'm inclined toward believing my mother, not because my father is inclined toward fallacy or hyperbole. Except my mother had (and has) no cleavage to speak of really. My mother is exceptionally beautiful, that's true, but an abundance of cleavage? No. Sorry. He remembers that moment as he's come to fondly wish (and believe) it was—imaginary cleavage and all.

But whatever really happened, who hit on whom, something clicked in that "other room" (with no real park view to speak of by the way—men and their tricks!).

Another fact? My father's then wife was in the next room over.

But that didn't matter so much. It was 1974 and let's just say that they were married in fiction but not fact. But I do like to joke that my father is the only man who really ever left his wife to marry the other woman. Making my mother the exception, not the rule.

Another fact? My parents say they went on their first date soon after that and they knew. That they were it. For each other. I'm sure it wasn't that simple. I'm sure there were fights and doubts. Insecurities to overcome and idiosyncrasies to accept. But they don't talk about that part. They talk about how they knew. Just knew.

My father formally divorced his first wife, my parents moved in together, and they were married a few years later in 1979. And they've been together ever since. Not always happily, but I think far more happy than not. They're certainly still (sickly) in love, and that they're partners in everything is clear. They're each other's best friend.

I can only guess that in some ways they're so fully combined at this point, it would be hard for me, as their child, to recognize those distinct individuals who met in 1969. Who those version of Margaret and Wayne were, I'm not sure. My guess is that my mother has grown stronger from my father's presence. That she's learned to trust in herself by virtue of someone else believing in her so fiercely. It must be said: My father is fierce. In everything he does. He's a lot of personality in a small package. So my guess is that my mother showed him how to be still, how to be subtle, to smooth the furrow in his brow, that it was okay to have a glass of wine on a weeknight. She rounded his edges. But those are just guesses.

Another guess is that they learned how to be a family together. Neither one had real examples from their childhoods of the kind of family they wanted to be. My mother's father died when she was young and her mother was emotionally unavailable, to put it mildly. My father's mother was his father's second *and* fourth wife. Enough said. So neither of my parents really knew how to be the couple they wanted to be—there was no modeling to look to. They had to figure it out on their own. How to really let another person love them, how to be generous, how to support and grow and stick together even when the instinct is to jet. They've figured it all out on their own.

For example, another fact is that when my parents met my mother didn't want to have children. My father did. But he believed that her desire to remain without kids was, in fact, a bluff. That it was apprehension of the unknown. And fear of perpetuating the mistakes made in her own childhood. He was patient. He let her come to the conclusion on her own. And then one day she had a dream about a baby playing on a beach in East Hampton. I was born about a year later.

Another thing I do know is that for both of them, theirs is the defining relationship of their lives. That they've never connected to anyone else, loved anyone else, like they do each other. That much I do know.

✳ ✳ ✳

Hannah Brown Gordon is a literary agent living in New York City, where, co-incidentally she also grew up and attended college. (Yes, she's aware most of her life has been lived in the same ten-mile radius. And, yes, she's fine with that.) She hopes to someday run a marathon, travel to Tasmania, and perfect the art of making piecrust.

martha and jim

by Kate Spencer

I HAVE A LETTER FROM MY MOTHER, written a month or so after she found out her body was home to a cancer spreading across every organ it touched. It's a short note, but heavy on the mom wisdom, and in it she offers this tidbit of advice:

"Be kind to your partner."

My parents met at a college party when they were barely eighteen years old. As the story goes, she was turned on by his soulful harmonica playing and he was smitten with her polished feet. For their first date my dad grilled them a trout he caught in the lake near his Massachusetts college, and their courtship consisted mostly of gatherings in the woods and hours spent sipping beer and laughing in the dorm room he shared with seven other kids on financial aid. They would hitchhike between each other's schools to spend time together, and married in a small ceremony when they were just twenty and twenty-one. They couldn't afford an engagement ring—they couldn't afford anything really—so my mom walked down the aisle wearing the cameo necklace my grandfather purchased for his mother while stationed in Italy in World War II. When I reached that age where kids become desperately obsessed with both material things and fitting in, I was mortified that my mom had no diamond ring to show for their union, like the other mothers I saw picking their kids up outside of my elementary school. I was too young, dumb, and enthralled with acceptance to realize that my parents just didn't give a shit about fancy, expensive things, and had yet to learn that not giving a shit made them pretty damn cool.

My mom and dad weren't really hippies (though my dad did leave his car on the side of the highway to get into Woodstock, and my mom's friend gifted them twenty joints as a wedding present) so much as they were just straight-up young and poor. With twenty-dollar wedding rings on their hands, they weaved their way up to Canada, a tent and a two-person sleeping bag serving as their honeymoon suite. There they snapped photos of themselves resting on their backs gazing fearlessly at the sun, my mom aimlessly fingering the necklace my dad had constructed for her out of shells and string. Back home in Boston, they moved into an apartment on the second floor of the married housing dorm while my dad finished up his senior year of college. They spent the early years of their marriage eating peas and pasta (a recipe passed down by the Italians in my family from one broke newlywed to the next) and watching "M.A.S.H" and "Saturday Night Live" on a small black-and-white TV.

They rarely spent money on each other, but for my parents, every moment together was an expression of love. Because they united at a time when they had nothing but each other they shared their love in simple ways, with handmade gestures of adoration and devotion—like the notes they left for each other around the house, day in and day out, for thirty-five years.

There were the practical notes—"The dishes in the dishwasher are clean"—and the notes that horrified my brother and me—"You're the most special person to me and my best friend." "Love you!—D" was the most common one, using the one-letter nickname they both shared for each other, the origin of which I've never been privy to. Most often the notes would live on the kitchen counter, but they also hid them for each other around the house, by the sink so the other would spot it while flossing, next to the coffeepot, or taped on the steering wheel of the car. Many drives to school began with my mom smiling at a note my dad had left, followed by her shrieking at us to buckle our seat belts. (Her Jeep still sits in the driveway of my childhood home, the side compartment overflowing with one-line notes from my dad.)

My mom's cancer diagnosis did nothing to deter their daily declarations of love and adoration, except that they often directed the notes at my brother and me, after we moved home to help with her care. Wander into my parents' kitchen and you'll find "Love you kiddies!" still taped on the wall next to the paper towels, a relic from an early-morning chemo appointment. When she was still well enough, my mom gave away all her jewelry to family and friends, with tiny little greetings attached to each box. As her health deteriorated and it became clear she was going to leave us, she'd sit up in bed, spending hours writing out lengthy instructions on how to operate the washer-dryer, or detailing the different lightbulbs we owned and their intended outlets. When she couldn't sleep, she'd wander the house plastering gadgets and cabinets with her personalized mom directions. Even her expensive La Mer face cream—her one splurge—was left with a Post-it note on top: "Don't use too much! Only need a small dab."

In the days after my mom died, appliance after appliance broke down—the furnace, the vacuum, the dryer, the dishwasher—and her pages of instruction, taped all over our home, quietly calmed our *how the fuck are we going to fix this!* panic.

It's clichéd to say that it's always about the little things, but over the years the little things grow into an enormous expression of who we are. My parents bestowed small acts of kindness upon each other that rooted our family in love. Consider this my thank-you note.

✻ ✻ ✻

Kate Spencer is a senior editor at VH1.com, where she manages the celebrity and entertainment blog TheFABlife.com. She teaches and performs long-form improv comedy at the Upright Citizens Brigade Theatre in New York and can be seen there each week with the group Reuben Williams. In addition to being a comedian and writer, Kate is also a certified yoga instructor—or, as her parents say, "unique." She lives in Brooklyn and lives online at KateLikesYou.com.

roger and terry

by Kyle Beachy

CAUTION, THEY SAY, TO THOSE WHO would trust a son or daughter on the subject of parents. We are too close, see, too *related* to be reliable. Part of this is egotism: Inside my privatized universe, this man and woman make a godly pair. To share their story is in a sense to narrate my own origin, a myth I could be compelled to glorify or downplay to any number of desired effects, depending on the audience. The second obstacle to consider is epistemological. They are, after all, our first celebrities, parents, whether in person or absentia. We know of their lives only through echo and shadow and reflection, a vast network of hearsay and legend.

And so: *caution.*

My mother's father was a gambler and my father was

born the son of a preacher man. They met in Goshen, Indiana, a quiet town, when she got up from the crowded coffee shop where she was studying and wandered into a quiet corner of a quiet campus building. Imagine, next, the echo of hard-soled shoes in the empty hallway. Did he follow her? Yes. Is this creepy, or romantic? Yes. And when he introduced himself, speaking simply with typical Mennonite respect, it was no longer creepy, and the very next day they would marry. Or if not technically the next day then very soon indeed, married at an age so young that it was and remains the least reasonable act they have committed. After college they relocated to pursue graduate study at Michigan State, and one day, outside of their apartment building outside of East Lansing, had their picture taken on the back of what appears to be a motorcycle.

A young, married ticklefest on the back of a motorcycle. This despite a lifelong (my life) opposition, adamant and tireless, to motorcycles.

Truth, here, is the vigor of the early '70s coded into their outfits and hair. Behind them stand two skeletal trees, a swing set, and the kind of fence over which one longs to vault. It is early evening. Their shadows grow longer. As for the occasion, it would appear nothing more than an evening out. Off to a meal, something sensible, or a concert. I imagine a sensible and subdued vocalist or, say, solo clarinetist. Sensible. The bond on display offers little room for confusion: the singular intimacy of man and woman straddling a common object. This is history itself, theirs and mine, a truth contained within the grainy image, revived by attention.

It was only a little put-put thing, my mother explains, definitely not a motorcycle.

For context and re: my older sister, she'll add, she was either pregnant or about to be, but I have already moved on, landing again on these two faces and what would seem to be the photograph's true occasion, which is joy. Mouth open, eyes shut: It is contagious. The blur of her right arm slipped free from his shoulder; meanwhile the left struggles with his bicep. Her shirt is loose and roomy; it settles over her body like a calm. Her hair is thick and dark and loosely curled. If I squint I see the earliest stages of what have become wrinkles, but for now her face is open wide, smooth, and young.

Meanwhile my father wears my mother like the world's lightest backpack, a helium lover. He also wears two distinct sets of vertical stripes. His hair is parted sweepingly as I've always known it, right to left, reassuring after the motorcycle. A tall man, Roger, a two-sport athlete and conscientious objector. A man who grew up on farms and continued farming in the laboratory. Unlike hers, his smile stays hidden inside shadow. But joy finds expression elsewhere.

Is it fall? spring? A silver sky hovers depthless over grass worn raw beneath the swings. Though you can't tell in the photo, her eyes are brown. He hunches forward with his long arms bent as if to protect some thing he unsecretly would like to lose—call it composure—while her hands grapple. I imagine them eating, in those days, a lot of sandwiches and soup. Young enough here to laugh this way, younger here than I am now. Which is to say: The now confronts the here, and marvels.

It's an apartment in Okemos, Michigan, just a few clicks east of East Lansing. They've come to Michigan State together, he for agriculture and she for speech pathology. These are facts. He would study plant life closely and devote his life to two goals: eliminating chemicals from our food and increasing yield in regions besot by viral infections and drought and hunger. She would work in hospitals and schools, watching closely the mouths of victims of trauma and disease, teaching speech through burps. She tells a story of the man in the ER because his tongue was injured. Turns out he tried to rape an eighty-year-old woman, who bit out a chunk of his tongue, saved it, and gave it to the police, so they could make a match at the hospital. An interesting place to work, she says of East St. Louis.

I attended my parents' wedding. That's another fact.

The photo's era, an age of analog everything, is the era of the music on which I was raised. When my mother visits my home I always put on Harry Nilsson or Willie Nelson, sometimes Mama Cass, and I cannot explain to you the joy I derive from brewing a cup of tea and sitting, listening. As a child I had a lisp of my own that she remedied. I was also, it sounds like, a sickly kid, prone to ear infections, and apparently a dumbshit as well: There's a story of the time I shoved a Gummi Bear into a nostril that stuck there and went rank. Now she flies to England to care for her mother, who is very very old, and frail, and small. Her father, Harry, has been dead for twenty-eight years.

My father's father, the Mennonite preacher, died on the road. He was driving homeward one evening along a divided highway in rural Ohio when a car traveling the opposite direction crossed the median. Two cars collide with not another for miles. Neil Beachy gave my father his nose, frame, and faith, the last of which fell into crisis following the crash. The other driver was a grade-school teacher who'd been drinking for several hours at a nearby tavern and on her way home decided to kill herself. His headlights, her solution, must have appeared out of the darkness as a kind of gift, perhaps an invitation from the very God my father was left to question.

My father's music is Dvorak and Tchaikovsky, the Romantics, with some Springsteen to round things out. The man his mother married six years after Neil's death has survived at least the following: having a house collapse onto him; having a house explode around and through him; and having the better part of his body's left side shattered when his Buick was struck by a driver who failed to see, or willingly ignored, a red light. The woman who decided to commit suicide by crossing the median that night also survived. These together, maybe, forming some kind of argument that it was God herself who gave us laughter.

My mother came to Goshen when her father, Harry, an English soldier, gambler, and spoon player, moved them from Bristol, England, to open a diner he would name, simply and factually, after himself. His own frequent laugh was a thing of legend, baroque and raspy. As a young woman my mother's mother spent the war ducking into backyard shelters during air raids. Knowle West is a neighborhood of two-story brick duplexes populated by mostly benevolent, except sometimes to one another, working families. She fried black-market eggs for her brothers and sisters, using black-market butter. When she married Harry her name became doubly colorful: Violet Brown. The daughter they brought along on the *Queen Mary* was seven years old, wide-eyed and round-faced. She stood at the railing and spoke excitedly of waves and motion in an accent that still reappears when a phone call comes from England.

She arrived at Goshen College midyear after spending the autumn after high school working at Harry's, saving enough to cover one semester at a time. Harry would not hear of credit or loans. And so Terry Brown appeared on campus during a gray late January, one more townie at the small, Mennonite liberal arts school she chose less for Anabaptist leanings than proximity. She was a dancer—a sock hopper, weekend stroller for whom dating meant doing fun things together, waterskiing for example, an age of quaint wonder. Dancing was forbidden at the school, or perhaps just discouraged. Accounts vary. She hung trays of burgers and fries on the windows of cars parked outside Harry's. I have said at least once before that my mother wore roller skates at the diner, but a recent email revealed this to be a lie.

Here's Mom and Dad on the (not a) motorcycle. Here are shadows. Her force and his counterforce. Analog everything—leave the boundaries to the digital, this or not this, while the analog remains a world of relations. But I'm frustrated by all that's missing. The photo already points backward to their lives before Okemos, Michigan. Why not forward as well? Is this so much to expect? Shouldn't it auger more clearly what stories come next?

When they got divorced, each of my parents began drinking. Not hard, but some. My mother spent time with a mustached man who had fingers like sausages and who I would surely have disliked had I ever successfully taken him seriously. My father dated within scientific circles, though I only knew them via snapshot encounters, brief and awkward. In those years he was living in San Diego and my sister was in college in Ohio. My mother and I shared a ground-floor unit in St. Louis. We were robbed at one point, and efficiently: They took only her jewelry and my Nintendo system and games. Insurance payouts allowed me to update to a Super NES and surely forced my mother to evaluate; each ring an emotion gone and potentially replaced.

A photograph's purpose is forensic, and staring is an act of reconstitution. The story it tells is both more and less reliable than what you'll hear from me. In my account, their story follows my own time line. They separated in seventh grade and remarried by the time I went to college. Remarried *each other,* please note, inside the chapel at the base of Copper Mountain, in Colorado. Meaning my parents have two anniversaries I manage to forget, an ongoing gag we're able, or at least I'm able, to laugh about.

Hers is the story of the English girl who grew up dancing in an American diner. His is the story of the Mennonite farm boy who did and does not like to dance, and eventually became the first to genetically modify a tomato to resist viral infection. Mine is the story of reading and writing theirs, my gratitude awesome.

✳ ✳ ✳

Kyle Beachy grew up in St. Louis and lives in Chicago, where he teaches writing and literature at the School of the Art Institute of Chicago, the University of Chicago's Graham School, and Roosevelt University. In the off season he teaches at the University of Iowa's Summer Writing Festival. His first novel, *The Slide,* was published by The Dial Press in 2009, and his short fiction and essays have appeared variously in print and online. He has received fellowships from the Bread Loaf Writers' Conference and the Danish Arts Council.

diane and michael

by Leigh Newman

IN 1971, MY PARENTS PACKED UP their lives and their VW station wagon, and boarded a ferry for Alaska. They had their four-week-old daughter with them in a backpack. They had a cooler of sandwiches and a thermos of coffee. They were coming from California, where the sun always shone and the backyards smelled of lemons.

Dad and Mom and their newborn slept outside on the ferry deck, in sleeping bags. All around them slept other twenty-five-year-olds with folk guitars and long hair and goatskin wine bags. The days passed—two, three, four. Glaciers shattered into the sea. Whales surfaced. The travelers shared their stories: Some were headed to Alaska to commercial fish, some to escape the IRS, some to trap beavers or pan for gold (no joke), some "just to be free."

Dad and Mom kept very quiet. They were coming due to a fluke in government paperwork. They were supposed to be stationed in New Mexico. My father was a doctor, working off his military time in the public health service in order to avoid being sent to Vietnam. My mother was a social worker, wearing a cashmere twin set and carrying a monogrammed beauty case filled with Aqua Net and eye shadow. She tried to sit with less-than-perfect posture. Dad tried to tell the drifters and dreamers and hippies not to cough or sneeze on the baby . . . without actually telling them this and being rude.

At the time, Alaska, the largest state in the Union, was home to less than 150,000 people. The big city of Anchorage was covered in a cloud of dust from all the unpaved roads, most of which simply ran out at the start of the mountains. The Garden of Eatin', the most popular restaurant in town, was housed in an old military Quonset hut and served green beans fresh from the can. There were no first-run movies or foreign car dealerships or department stores except for JCPenney. At night, my parents lay in bed listening to the walls of their apartment shake—not from earthquakes but from moose ramming their antlers into the side of the building, looking for food.

The first week of August, they decided to celebrate the move with a picnic to Portage Glacier, a famous tourist site outside of town. The sun was out, the rivers throbbing with salmon. The wide blue glacier slabbed down between the mountains. At the base lay a viewing area. Mom spread out a blanket and sat down with *Hawaii,* a Michener novel. Dad slung the baby into the backpack and went for a hike. There was no actual trail up the mountain, but he picked his way up the boulders and loose shale.

He climbed a little higher, then a little higher. He came to a snow patch and crossed it. Then another snow patch. It was pretty cool, actually to be crossing snow in the middle of summer, the sun hot on his back, his little baby babbling in his ear. Below, people were waving at him. He stopped and waved back. Wow, he thought, Alaskans sure are friendly!

He moved along the snow patch, whistling, worrying about sunburn from the glare. He looked down again. More people were waving at him, gathered around the base of the mountain. Maybe waving on mountains was like waving on fishing boats, he thought, you waved to be a good sportsman. He waved again. They waved again—the whole crowd of speck-people. Some of them, in fact, were waving with both hands and jumping up and down.

Hhmm.

Dad worked his way down the snow patch. Maybe the people were cheering him on, he thought. Maybe nobody had ever climbed this mountain before, especially with a baby. He moved a little farther down, a little farther. People were screaming at him now, turning red-faced. He could hear them even.

"Get off the glacier! Get off the glacier!"

Because, as Dad found out, snow at the top of an Alaskan mountain isn't always snow. It's pretty frequently a glacier. A glacier that moves. A glacier that hides, under a two-inch rind of snow, yawning deep crevasses, one of which Dad and the baby should have fallen into, never to be seen again.

Saved by luck or good footing, he flopped back down on the picnic blanket. "Did you two have fun, honey?" Mom asked, looking up from her novel. She'd been so engrossed, she'd missed all the commotion.

One month later, the hospital called. Dad had never shown up for work. Mom threw the baby in the car and drove through town, frantic, searching for him. Had he crashed? Had a bear in the parking lot eaten him? She found Dad standing on the side of the one major road in Anchorage, taking pictures of the Chugach Mountains—the foothills sheathed in purple fireweed, the peaks sloped in September snow. Dad had been so engrossed in the scenery, he'd forgotten about his job.

The baby girl in Dad's backpack and Mom's car was me. As an adult, I've never been sure how memory works. Do we remember what's most telling about our lives? Or is everything telling, once we look at it knowing how things turned out? Either way, the two events seem to have a certain resonance—one parent fascinated by the beauty of a novel, one parent fascinated by the beauty of the wilderness.

For the next forty years, Dad would remain in Alaska flying airplanes, hunting caribou, and fly-fishing for salmon. Mom would leave the state, heading back to the East Coast in search of book clubs and art museums. On the deck of that ferry, they were not dreaming of moose and snow and mountains. But moose and snow and mountains happened to them. And they used the experience to figure out how they wanted to live for the rest of their lives, facing up to truths about themselves and their marriage that nobody ever wants to face—which, in my opinion, was the real adventure. It's always the real adventure, whether it happens in Alaska or Kansas, Manhattan or Bakersfield.

✳ ✳ ✳

Leigh Newman's memoir about growing up in Alaska will appear from Dial/Random House in 2011. Her fiction and nonfiction have appeared in *One Story*, *Tin House*, *The New York Times*' Modern Love column, and on National Public Radio's *The Sound of Writing*. She has received fellowships from the Corporation of Yaddo, the Edward Albee Institute, and the University of Massachusetts–Amherst.

kevin and moira

by Ben Craw

IT WAS COLD, IT WAS RAINY, and it was well past midnight. But it was also their wedding night. Giving up was simply not an option.

So the young newlyweds Kevin and Moira Craw (and I mean *young*—twenty and twenty-one, respectively) drove on through the night, wending their way along dark, icy, heavily wooded New England back roads in search of . . . well, okay, let's just be blunt here: They were looking for a place to get it on.

The original plan—a lovely nocturnal furlough of secluded connubiality at the elegantly rustic Silvermine Tavern of Norwalk, Connecticut—had been abandoned following a period of knocking on/peering into locked doors and pitch-black windows and then the eventual realization that nobody was waiting up to greet them and that the old country inn was, in fact, very closed. "We were laughing a lot," my dad recalls. "It was just very dark."

It made perfect sense, of course. My dad had made the reservation days beforehand but hadn't thought to inquire about hours or alert any personnel to the possible schedule permutations of the big night. My parents had never even booked their own hotel room before. Did I mention they were twenty?

My dad's mother, Patty, in her typically near-clairvoyant wisdom, seemed to foresee it all. All night she had been gently urging my parents to make their gracious exit from the reception party at her house in Westport ("Aren't you kids eager to be alone? Hm?"), no doubt hopeful that their wedding night would be more . . . successful than hers had been. Patty married my grandpa Jim during a brief leave from his duties as an officer during World War II. Due to some unfortunate timing of a certain twenty-eight-day female physiological cycle, Jim wasn't permitted to lay a hand on Patty on their wedding night and had to report back to duty before getting the chance. So Patty's anxiety wasn't without merit. (Of course, some of it may have also been due to the [mis]conception that it would be her son and daughter-in-law's "first time.") But my parents were young and just married. They wanted to hang out and party with their friends.

So there they were, sitting in the remote darkness outside the inn. By now it was about one in the morning. My folks weren't exactly familiar with the full spectrum of the region's late-night hospitality offerings. On top of that, they were twenty. And students. To wit: completely broke. It was March 1972, and while credit cards had been invented by then, my old man sure as hell didn't have one. What he had was forty, maybe fifty dollars in his pocket and not a clue what to do with it.

That's when my mom remembered the name of a place her older brother had once stayed: the Hi-Ho Motel.

"It was like a lodge for hunters and fishermen," Mom foggily suggests when I ask her to describe it. "No," Dad assures me. "It was a place for shiftless itinerants to stop and screw." Mom concedes: "Yeah, it was a dump. And we knew it."

But it met all the critical requirements of proximity (close) and cost (utterly cheap), and at one in the morning with no alternatives and no prospects, there wasn't much choice for my parents but to swallow hard and say, "Let's go Hi-Ho."

They weren't entirely confident in their direction as they drove along the winding, unlit Merritt Parkway. But eventually from behind the crest on the horizon came rising up the towering, glowing red, and perpetually one-block-letter-short beacon: HI-HO MOT L.

When they dinged the bell at the front desk, the attendant ignored them in favor of the mini TV playing behind the counter. It wasn't until the commercial break that the man finally glanced up. My mom, attempting to establish legitimacy and dignity, conspicuously flashed her brand-new ring. "As if the guy gave a rat's shit," remarks Dad.

There was, as a matter of fact, a champagne and fruit basket "upscale package," and you goddamn better believe my old man sprung for it. "I didn't wanna look cheap in the Hi-Ho," he tells me. "C'mon man, I was flashin' cash! Payin' the costs to be the boss!" The total charge came to $22.50.

Key in hand, my parents ventured down the hall to their room. Of course, the key didn't work. So: back to the front desk, bell, ding, and once more stand and wait for the commercial break on the mini TV. Then:

Dad: "The key doesn't work."

Man: "Uh, oh yeah. That was the room that got broken into. They changed the locks."

Around this time the man apparently experienced a twinge of pity for my parents, so upon finding a key to another room he walked them down the hall and opened the door himself. At which point the man turned to my father and said: "All night long, square. Knock yourself out."

Kinda spoiled the romance of carrying the bride over the threshold, but hey—welcome to the Hi-Ho.

The walls were cracked. The bed sagged. The carpets didn't match up. But lacking the energy to complain, my parents just sat down and laughed. They fed quarters into the bed's Magic Fingers machine: no movement, just a loud grinding noise, "like a rock crusher," Dad says. "So all you really got was the thrill of what the neighbors must be thinking."

Nevertheless, it was their wedding night. So my parents found some towels and laid them over the discolored, mildewed pillows. What ensued is described alternately by my father as "a brief interlude," and by my mother as "the quickest fuck of all time." (I apologize to everyone, primarily myself, for writing that. But the quote is verbatim.) "If I weren't twenty there is no way I could've gotten aroused," Dad tells me. Mom asserts it was entirely he who forced the issue. Dad's stance: "I think she was a hellcat looking for love. She says I was a horndog who would not be denied. That's what you call memory." In any case. Marriage: consummated.

Just a few short hours later, my parents awoke to the clanging sounds of predawn fishermen outside their window. With the fear of another break-in forefront in their minds, they decided sleeping in was a luxury they couldn't afford. "Our eyes popped open and we just thought, *Let's get the hell out of here.*"

It was about six thirty in the morning when my parents staggered half conscious into the kitchen. Patty was already awake, doing dishes from the night before. She took one look at the bedraggled couple and felt a wave of dread. Something had gone wrong. Had my father been abusive? Had my mother suddenly discovered she didn't like men? Had they experienced a repeat of her own wedding night misfortune?

"What's the matter?" Patty cried.

"It's a long story."

In March 2010 my parents celebrated their thirty-eighth wedding anniversary. The Hi-Ho Motel is still standing. But they opted instead for a quiet dinner at home.

✳ ✳ ✳

Ben Craw is a writer and Web video producer covering national politics and media for *The Huffington Post*. He previously worked at *Talking Points Memo*. Ben grew up in Wilton, Connecticut, where his once awesome parents still live.

Pete

by Holly Peterson

MY DAD DIDN'T REALLY LIKE TO smoke or drink. Unfortunately, in 1946, the rest of the country was really in the mood to smoke and drink after everything the world had been through. My father's MIT fraternity brothers at Alpha Tau Omega thought they should give him a hard time with his non-bacchanalian preferences; maybe even try to change his ways. So the first thing they did was lock him in a closet with a foot-long cigar and decide not to let him out until he finished it.

His older fraternity brothers preferred paddles with little holes in them because they grabbed his bare rear end flesh and caused bigger welts. And of course they made my father drink way too much when he had no taste for it in the first place. I've probably seen my father drink a glass of red wine ten times in my entire life, and he doesn't even finish it. In college, he was more the studious type than the lady-killer type so the "brothers" also thought it would be a great idea for him to get the G-string of the most famous stripper in Boston, Sally Keith.

In this photo, he was just home from college, fresh from acquiring that G-string, not by sexual conquest, but by way of pleading at the back entrance of the stripper club. He was visiting his Greek immigrant parents, George and Venetia Peterson, in his hometown of Kearney, Nebraska. (At Ellis Island, Petropoulos was changed to Peterson.)

Kearney was a small but famous town because if you measured the exact midpoint between the East and West coasts of the country, the tip of your pin would touch Kearney, 1,733 miles to Boston and 1,733 miles to San Francisco. My grandparents had run the Central Café restaurant in the center of Kearney, just off the railroad tracks, once they got settled in the new country. You could get a hot beef sandwich with mashed potatoes and a piece of pie for dessert for thirty cents in the mid-1940s. This establishment catered to the air force men on the base nearby and to the families who lived in Kearney full-time. The Central Café stayed open twenty-four hours a day for twenty-seven years under the strict and thrifty rule of my grandfather George. On the bathroom towel containers, a sign read, WHY USE TWO WHEN ONE WILL DO? On the night they decided to close the Central Café at midnight for the first time in almost three decades, my grandfather found himself outside trying to lock up only to realize he didn't even have a key because he'd never once needed one.

My father tells me at this point in his life he was hoping to become a businessman after graduation. "Everyone was optimistic in those days, no one had any trouble finding jobs." He later worked on the Eisenhower campaign as head of marketing in the Midwest. Though he certainly wasn't the person who came up with the "I Like

Ike" slogan, he remembers discussing how simple it was, how true it was, and how everyone thought it might just stick.

I wonder how much he worried about his ability to find success in life at this stage, in this photograph. Did he know he would become one of America's great self-made men? He was studying business at this time, but what would he have said if some lady with a crystal ball told him he'd serve as US Secretary of Commerce or steer and form some of the great firms on Wall Street—he would become CEO of Lehman Brothers and later start up the Blackstone Group from scratch. What would he have said if this clairvoyant told him he would be receiving phone calls from US presidents wanting his take on America's economic woes? Or that iconic corporate chieftains like Warren Buffett or Jack Welch would be trading barbs and jokes with him, not to mention seeking his advice? I know he never would have believed her.

Most overachievers are never satisfied with their accomplishments. My father is an extremely confident man, but I would say he is never satisfied with his success and always needs to keep pushing forward on that front, even as an octogenarian.

He always talks about his own parents. How hard they worked, how they were the embodiment of the American dream, how they saved every penny to enable their own sons to have a better future than they did. He admired them for giving back to the men who knocked on the back door of the Central Café hungry and tired. His father would feed them, only after putting them to work for a few hours to preserve their dignity.

My dad is all about dignity, all about living out the dream his parents had for him. Coming from immigrant parents, growing up in the Dust Bowl during the Depression, he doesn't like anything flashy. So living his dream isn't living a hedonistic dream, it's living a life of working in a hard, but fulfilling, job and giving back.

My father's upbringing in the Depression defines so much about how he behaves today. He can't stand wasting food, leaving the lights on, or, God forbid, missing a sale. Though he left Blackstone, he is now busy donating the bulk of his fortune to his foundation devoted to remedying America's fiscal problems. He would never be able to live with himself otherwise.

As I had my first child, someone once told me that children do as you do, not as you say. My father is always intentionally setting an example through what he does. He's now in his early eighties and still working like a dog every day, still never wasting one moment and so writing speeches in the dentist's chair (and driving the dentist with drill in hand crazy), and still obsessing over charts and graphs that monitor our economy until late in the night. I can't say I work as hard as he does, but I do intrinsically enjoy my job and the sense of accomplishment I get though my professional life, and I am very much attuned to his values about work. Because we share so many interests and have traveled the world together several times over on fact-finding missions to places like Cuba, Kazakhstan, Kuwait, and Vietnam, we are very close. He's always teasing, and likes to feign disgust at my supposed yuppie, boomer lifestyle. But those of us on the inside know he only teases those he loves the most.

Pete Peterson is not real big on giving himself a break, perhaps one key to his success. I guess he learned some of that from his own parents. When he was thirty-four years old and had just won an award as one of the youngest presidents in America running a Fortune 300 company (the camera company Bell and Howell), he went home for a visit to Kearney and went for a walk on this very sidewalk. His own parents earnestly said to him, "Petey, you sure you want to get involved in that company and have to deal with all kinds of people and their demands? Why don't you come home to stay and you can run your own business, the Central Café?"

✳ ✳ ✳

Holly Peterson is a *New York Times* bestselling fiction author and a con-
tributing editor at *Newsweek* magazine. She worked for a decade at ABC
News, where she won an Emmy for her coverage of the fall of the Soviet
Union. She also worked as an editor at large for *Talk Magazine.* Her work
has been published in *Talk, Newsweek, The New York Times,* and *Vogue.*
She has three children.

Martin

by Bradley H. Gendell

EVERY THANKSGIVING MY UNCLE MARTIN would visit my family in Cincinnati from New York City, arriving like a nor'easter, bringing a blast of sophistication to our suburban home. Mornings were for lounging in the silk pajamas and robes that earned him his first nickname, "Uncle P.J." Evenings called for one or two martinis—always Beefeater with a twist, sometimes over ice and sometimes not—which earned him his second nickname, "Uncle Martini." In total, his good looks and stylish clothes, taste for good food and drink, and skills as a conversationalist and raconteur implied that his life was a constant stream of glamorous parties, receptions, and restaurants. Years later, when I moved to New York myself, I learned that it was all true.

Even as he grew older, Uncle Martin stayed single, childless, and forever young. At age seventy-three, when his peers were retiring to Florida, Martin went to Burning Man.

This was the Uncle Martin I knew from his visits during my youth, from my own early days as a bachelor when he showed me around New York, through his untimely passing at the age of seventy-six.

It wasn't until he was gone, through conversations with his old friends and by discovering a treasure trove of old photos in his spare apartment, that a younger, and even more awesome version of Uncle Martin came to life: a 1950s rake, a ringleader of a band of pranksters with a taste for capers and escapades. It was obvious that these were not your typical collegiate parties—which one of my own college roommates described simply as "a keg and a lot of cups"— these were major happenings with themes, traditions, performances, and guest appearances. It was theater and Uncle Martin was the director, producer, and star.

A good student, Martin left his boyhood home in Ossining, New York, to attend the University of Chicago, where he began meeting some of the people who shaped our culture in the years to come— he encountered Mike Nichols, Elaine May, and Philip Glass. He was also introduced to a men's magazine that got its start in Chicago in 1953: *Playboy.*

Martin was an active member of the Beta Theta Pi fraternity, whose members served as both witnesses and accomplices to his antics. In 1955, Beta House threw one of the first college parties to feature an appearance by a live *Playboy* playmate. After making the arrangements, Martin and his good friend Chuck drove to the original Playboy Mansion in Chuck's old Pontiac. They picked up a Playmate to make an appearance at the party (the pretty blonde in the picture) and returned her safely, in Chuck's words, "at 0 dark

100 hours." The photos that survive show a rocking party replete with booze, singing, pretty girls, well-groomed young men, a Jaguar roadster, and a giant two-story banner of a well-dressed rabbit holding a champagne glass. In one photo Uncle Martin is pouring champagne playfully into the rabbit's coupe from a second-story window.

On another occasion, Martin was in charge of supplying liquor to an inter-fraternity council party. The party was in a suite at the Shoreham Hotel where outside liquor was prohibited. Undeterred, Martin and his sidekick Chuck donned suits and ties, pretended they were chemical salesmen with "samples" for a "trunk show," and moved the liquor from Chuck's new Mercury to the suite.

When it came time for my uncle to enlist in the army, his Beta brothers threw him an all-night pre-induction party with characteristic abandon. Martin arrived at the Army Induction Center in Chicago's Loop at dawn, in the dead of winter, still in his tuxedo and propped up between two of his brothers. The sergeant threatened a court-martial on the spot.

After the army, the movable feast continued at Wharton Business School in Philadelphia. Lacking a fraternity, Martin made some new friends and rented a house at 106 38th Street, which they renamed "Club 106." The Club had a jam-packed party every Saturday night—one-dollar contribution for refreshments—and its own flag. On the night of Penn's inter-fraternity ball, Club 106 had its own gala: black tie, dinner, and enough champagne for each couple to have two bottles.

Early on the night of the "106 Ball," Martin commented that for all the best parties he could remember, he ended up sleeping in his tuxedo. That night, they all slept in their tuxedos and began a tradition that everyone in their circle sleep in their tuxedos after a big night out.

Uncle Martin died suddenly, after an infection in his heart caused cardiac failure. It was terrible to witness—I was with him daily over the two and half weeks of his illness—but given the sudden onset and short duration, it was the death he would have wanted. Just before he fell ill, he was working out at the gym daily and had packed a bag (with a tuxedo, of course) to attend a family wedding that weekend. He was not quite the handsome dandy of his youth, but he was slim and stylish and coiffed until the very end.

As my sister Carin and I shared the sad chores of cleaning his apartment and informing his many friends, we likely learned more about Uncle Martin than we had in years. Many of the things we learned related to this particular time in his life when he was a young gadabout, but there were other things we learned, too. Carefully filed away was every wedding invitation, baby announcement, and bar or bat mitzvah *yarmulke* stretching back to his own parents' wedding. Who knew that our rakish uncle was so sentimental about family? One close friend of his told me how often he spoke about me ("You were like a son to him") and his excitement over the birth of our twins, one named after his father and the other after his brother, my father Gerald. These were thoughts he never shared with me directly, but I am happy to know he derived so much happiness from our family and that he had good friends in whom he confided.

Uncle Martin, I wish we had gotten to know some of this before you were gone, but as the closest thing you had to a son, I want you to know that you were awesome.

✻ ✻ ✻

Bradley H. Gendell is a former financial journalist who now works as an investor. He had his own career as a rakish bachelor, but now lives in New York with his wife and twin son and daughter, who he hopes, someday, will realize that he was once awesome.

addie and james

by Meg Federico

WHILE CLEARING OUT MY MOTHER'S HOUSE after her death in 2002, I found a folder of love letters from Dad in the early years of their marriage. Dad's first marriage had ended in divorce, a scandal in 1939—all the more because he got custody of his two young children. My mother, his second bride, was age twenty-four to his thirty-eight.

Dutiful and considerate spouses, I never imagined my parents *in love*. Even accounting for a child's immunity to parental chemistry, my father was not remotely alluring, at least not by the time I came along. Dad was substantial, a financial success, and *fifty*—about *seventy* in today's currency. My school friends assumed he must be my grandfather when introduced.

Other guys in Dad's category aquired three tuxedos,

two houses, an expensive bag of clubs, and a year-round tan. Not my dad, though he could have. Blind in the one eye, desperately myopic in the other, he wore leisure garb that did not include tennis whites or yachting ensembles. Instead, he wore an old buttondown shirt, the tails hanging out of the baggy shorts—his white, hairless legs exposed. A dish towel made a lump in the pocket. The perfect outfit for kneeling in the dirt to thin a row of seedling carrots. Not possibly a candidate for Cupid's arrow.

My mother, brainy, charming, and self-possessed (though she occasionally played against type for effect), was surely beyond Cupid's reach. With one hand, she would snatch that clichéd arrow out of the air and snap it over her knee. Yet the letters, and that she'd kept them, indicated otherwise.

I was in kindergarten, Dad grunted, shoring up a row of peas. He let me bang pegs into the ground, then he stretched strings from the top of the fence and knotted them on the pegs. Carefully, we wrapped the tendrils of young pea vines around the strings. "Now they'll climb up on their own," he told me, extracting the dish towel to mop his sweaty face. We planted lettuce, corn, zucchini, and a crazy patch of nasturtiums just for fun.

But I was a grown-up, staring at the end of my first marriage, when Dad spoke of his first: "She was unfaithful. But I neglected her, left her too much alone, let the business come first," he said, sighing. "A marriage takes tending."

The daily world of my parent's lives was as unimaginable as their sex appeal. A month or two after Dad married my mother, he hit the road—the railroad—because clinching a deal required a face-to-face handshake at conventions, central offices, even the homes of clients.

My father must have shuddered as he left his second bride—and sudden stepmother to *his* children—to manage alone.

When his first wife left him, Dad had returned early from just such a business trip because one of his eyes was giving out. He was dramatically rushed into surgery and was lying, post-op, in a darkened room, his eyes bandaged, his head immobilized by sandbags (standard protocol in those days), when he learned she had departed for a secret destination and had taken the kids. If he moved, if he even shed a tear, he risked losing the sight in the bad eye.

The operation was a failure.

Mindful of the past, he sent my mother one, two letters each day to ward off her loneliness or feeling of neglect. " I miss you so much. I am heart-broken not to be with you . . . ," he wrote from the train. "You mean a great deal to me now, but as the years go by, each year will bring a deeper meaning, and an even more satisfying one. You have all my faith and confidence . . ." Between the lines, *Don't leave.*

From the Drake Hotel in Chicago: "I think of you all the time. The old restlessness and impatience with the course of life that used to haunt me is all gone . . ." En route to Texas: "All the time on the train, I kept thinking that my next trip would be with you and it was a pleasant secret thought to have, while I was talking with only a part of my mind to the others . . ." Upon arrival in Houston: "The Shamrock Hotel is a fabulous place . . . a radio in every bedroom. Darling, you are just plainly the finest girl in the world. I admire and love you so much, and I miss you more than this pen can put down . . ."

From the Read House, in Chattanooga; the Dixie-Carlton in Birmingham; from the Frisco lines among St. Louis, Tulsa, and Oklahoma City, Dad diligently delivered affirmations of love. "It is almost incredible how deeply you have entered my life and heart . . . so very wonderful to me."

Of course, generating all that copy took effort, and sometimes, the material ran a little thin. The Drake Hotel, Chicago: "Darling, I developed a fine perspiration and got on the train dripping wet and a bit goatish . . ." From the train: "Dinner last night was punk—roast beef brown as leather, potatoes like lumps of laundry soap, string beans that must have been sent over from a rubber factory . . ."

If I had ever wondered why Dad preferred scratching out a meager backyard harvest to swanning around hot spots, I found my answer in his own words. The Boca Raton Club, Florida: " . . . a lovely place, but overpowering in size. I can never feel quite comfortable about so much display, eating, and pure pleasure seeking . . . You know I am happiest when I am with you at home."

Mom, over time, encouraged Dad to be more adventurous, and one summer she rented a villa in Italy with orchards and a private beach, sight unseen. Well, the "mansion" was in a subdivision, an awkward house cut up into many tiny bedrooms. The "orchards" consisted of three hastily planted saplings—peach, pear, and plum—that dried out and died during our month's tenancy. The beach was public, a ten-minute hike through the center of town.

Dad and I got the vegetable patch going, and then left it untended to day-trip around Italy from our rackety rented "mansion." We returned home to find weeds thriving in our garden, the tomatoes shriveled, rotting on the ground. But an infant pumpkin vine we'd left behind had crept through the garden fence to curl itself up a nearby tree. From a branch hung a small, perfect pumpkin round as the moon it was framed by the sky.

Dad's letters become less frequent, replaced by phone calls, train travel eclipsed by plane flights. The Shamrocks and the Drakes were bought out by chains like Hilton. Business became less personal, and more strategic. By the time Dad sold the company, international conglomerates were standardizing the financial and commercial landscapes. By the time he died, there was no trace left of the family firm he'd built, nor the business culture of friendships and handshakes that had made him a success.

After his death, Mom had the garden sodded over, an odd patch of lawn surrounded by a fence. She moved, even remarried. But the letters that went from his hand to hers were now, old and brittle, in mine. "I feel I am in your presence when I write to you," Dad wrote to my mother. And paging through the folder, I feel the love that grew between them and endured, so carefully tended when young, so warm even now.

✳ ✳ ✳

Meg Federico is a journalist, writer, and speaker based in Nova Scotia, Canada, though she considers herself a New Yorker. She is the author of the memoir *Welcome to the Departure Lounge: Adventures in Mothering Mother* (Random House, 2009).

dolores

by Durga Chew-Bose

I.

OUR POTATO KNEES MATCH AS WE SIT side by side on the
couch, peeling clementines and watching *Coronation
Street*. The radio is on in the kitchen and we've left the
balcony door open, and I can hear our tablecloth flapping
in the wind on the laundry line outside. Our upper du-
plex is shaded by the giant maple tree out front, and yet
we still sweat matching sweat beads on our noses. Like my
potato knees and dry skin, my sweaty nose was something
that once embarrassed me. When the episode ends and
the credits roll—the same slice-of-life song that for years
has trickled out of our television, a plaintive, reticent
tune—I stand up and cup my hands, offering to throw
away my mother's clementine peels. We share a brief and
unexpected smile, both quiet and wonderful, and yet

somehow dire. As if anchored by a memory, or the threat of forgetting, I sit back down beside her and rest my head on her lap as she plays with my hair. She reminds me about something I did as a child; the clementine peels warming in my palms.

II.

For restorative purposes, my mother still makes the same fruitcake recipe each Christmas. Briefly, our home smells like a memory and all is forgotten, and the sound of batter licking the side of that yellow plastic bowl is truly captivating. I catch her stealing glances of the old Time-Life recipe book and then of me, two fixed and memorized parts of her life that she still anxiously peeks at. As if she'd ever forget to pack the exact measure of brown sugar or add the dried currants, or forget to ask me about my boyfriend, or if I needed to buy shampoo or toothpaste before leaving in a week. My mother will never forget that recipe, and though at first the tiny scar on my forehead appears fresh, "Is that new? What happened?" she quickly remembers how furiously I scratched my chicken pox as a kid. Those scars, like the half cup of candied cherries, the shelled almonds, and the loaf pan lined with waxed paper waiting on the stovetop, have always been there.

III.

Listening to your mom remember her first pair of bell-bottoms or how growing up in Kolkata, she and her sisters would copy patterns from US *Vogue,* is a like being told a psychic secret that finally invites you to a daughters' club you naïvely sought membership to, the product of cable TV, Susan Sarandon mothers, Winona Ryder daughters, and sleepovers at friends' houses. In imagining my mother as impressionable and adolescent, perhaps a bit lithe with her new hips and small waist, and younger than I am now, I learned about nostalgia, borrowing it and misusing it. Listening to her delight in, recall, and sometimes misstep while singing along to my

Diana Ross CD often confused those maternal lines that for so long had been much clearer.

IV.

At my cousin's wedding years ago, my mother did the twist in her sari. She put out imaginary cigarettes with the balls of her heels and with her toes—she got real low. I stood against the wall next to my brother and felt for the first time a fiery sense of pride. As if baiting the rock and roll from them, a circle of clapping, cheering guests surrounded my parents. My mother was electric, possessed, and polished with pink and yellow disco lights. She was entirely swept by the music, summoning moves that effortlessly returned. Her head rolled back and forth, her lipstick was faded, her cheeks were round and red. Nobody knew my parents were separated.

I drank cherry Coke after cherry Coke that night and fell asleep in the hotel with my wedding clothes on. I imagine my mother in front of the bathroom mirror, unwrapping her sari as I slept and folding it flawlessly pleat by pleat so as not to get it wrinkled on the flight home.

V.

Along with papier-mâché stars and bobbles from India, and ornaments we made in school as children, Happy Meal toys from McDonald's—Bugs Bunny, a plastic train engine, a monster from a movie I cannot remember—once hung on our Christmas tree. My mother used to pull out her sewing kit and tie thread around Donald Duck's tail and Marvin the Martian's helmet, and my brother and I would find the right spot to hang our little toys. If a toy was too heavy, the branch would dip and mope. From the couch my mother could eye a stronger one and direct us to it, her field of focus shifting from tying tiny knots to scouting sturdy branches. Stevie Nicks, U2, Whitney Houston, and Run-DMC were caroling on our record player, and the mischievous and saddling idea that our gifts were hidden around the house was omnipresent.

I can distinctly remember the year when I no longer wanted our toys on the tree. Similarly, I wanted white twinkle lights instead of our rainbow ones. I preferred our more traditional ornaments: the gold ones, wooden ones, angel ones. Left in a box marked DECORA-TIONS, our Happy Meal toys with cartoon eyes and Cheshire smiles were no longer a part of Christmas. I am embarrassed by the list of things I have asked my mother to change. It's terrifyingly easy to rekindle that feeling of complete shame.

VI.

Deep inside our hallway linen closet and tucked beside our hand towels and faded neon beach towels, my mother used to store her extra boxes of sandalwood soap. Each bar was in an individual box—green with white patterns and red block letters—and each was imported from India in our suitcases, or an aunt's suitcase, or a friend of a friend's suitcase, along with guava jam and *sandesh*. The smell was so distinct and nearly potent and I remember thinking it was "acquired" like wine or strong cheese. It was nothing like lavender, vanilla, chamomile, or jasmine. But my mother loved it; she always has. And watching her mind and luxuriate in its specific smell is more intimate than most things, like witnessing a secret through the slim crack of a door left ajar.

✳ ✳ ✳

Durga Chew-Bose graduated from Sarah Lawence College in 2009. Her plans waver depending on the day, the season, or a conversation, but never stray far from her impulse to write it all down. For now, she lives in Brooklyn.

terry and kathy

by Brandy Barber

THERE'S A FAMOUS PAT CONROY NOVEL called *The Great Santini* that features an arrogant but memorable patriarch by the name of Bull Meecham. Bull, played by the great Robert Duvall in the movie adaptation, refers to his children as "shit birds" and puts his US Marine service above all else—including showing his family affection. My father, Terry, always loved to quote it, and jokingly referred to himself as The Great Santini. As a retired naval officer, and the son of a decorated army officer, he had a love of the story that was borne out of his experiences as both a son and father involved in the armed services. His wife, my mother Kathy, would laugh and agree with him heartily. When I was a teenager, I remember obtaining a paperback copy of Conroy's novel and enjoying it. But I had to disagree respectfully with my father and mother—

he was no Bull Meecham. My dad is one of the most loving, respectful, and humorous people I've ever met. And his wife is no small potatoes, either.

My mother was also the daughter of an army officer—in fact, my folks met because they lived next door to each other on the same army base in Washington State. I have the awesome legacy of having not only a family where all my aunts and uncles know one another, but one where they hung out together as teenagers and went to the same high schools. I always assumed everyone's family was so close, and had shared memories going back that far.

My whole life, military memorabilia has been around. Replicas of naval jets, flight suits, bullets mounted on engraved plaques, embroidered leather bomber jackets, American flags, ceremonial swords, all were mounted and displayed in the houses I grew up in and still feature prominently in my Dad's dark wood den. When the movie *Top Gun* came out, my dad wore his flight jacket to go see it in the theater with some of his airline pilot buddies, who all wore theirs as well. I was in my girlie-girl phase—obsessed with replacing the then eleven-year-old pre–Black Eyed Peas Fergie on *Kids, Incorporated* according to my diary—so I observed this with mild interest, mostly because I got to stay home that night and get my very own Domino's pizza. But when the buzz about the movie became huge, enough to hit the playground, I was none too slow to brag about my naval pilot dad to my classmates, especially the boy I had a crush on (who had just referred to me as a flat-chested baboon, natch).

As I got older and more political by way of reading *Bloom County* cartoons, I became obsessed with the Beatles and '60s counterculture. Now, I know most people like to share a lively tale about how their parents smoked the odd joint in college, but I am here to tell you my parents missed the '60s. They just said no to drugs—my dad was in ROTC in college and went directly into Officer Candidate School to be a pilot when most people were hotboxing in their broken-down VW vans. My mom was a high school mathematics teacher, busy at work getting death threats from Klan members in a school that was being desegregated. My parents were wary of my half-assed angry teen venture into this lifestyle, even though it was largely suggested to me by incense I purchased from Sam Goody in the local shopping mall. They even allowed me to wear a tie-dyed tank top emblazoned with a giant black peace sign on it, a fashion statement that I felt would solve all the world's problems. Bull Meecham would have probably hung me off the family's driveway basketball hoop with said garment. Even though it was, frankly, disrespectful to my father and both of my grandfathers' service, my parents let me make my own choices to wear that shirt. It occurred to me many years later how hard that must have been for my dad when we attended the Miramar Air Show, and I felt like a royal jackass.

Another amazing thing about having two relatively conservative parents and being a flaming liberal is that my parents never forced us to be religious. If I wanted to go to church—say, attend Sunday school after a friends' sleepover—they were okay with it. If I had never set foot inside a church to this day, they also would be supportive. I'm really amazed by this, as they have always made it clear that I and my brother (himself a naval pilot and decorated graduate of Annapolis) were able to choose what worked for us, spiritually. Add to this the fact that my mom has always worked outside of the home with my dad's blessing, which shows their very gender-equitable attitude, and I have to say my parents were some pretty amazing folks. I admire them more than they could ever know for being fair, kind, and totally encouraging of my individuality—even at the expense of theirs. They're no shit birds, that's for sure.

Brandy Barber is a writer, producer, and comedian. She lives with her husband, two cats, and a roller-skate collection in Brooklyn (www.brandybarber .com).

jim and kathy

by Jennifer E. Smith

MAYBE NOT ALL GREAT LOVE STORIES begin in a bar.

But this one does.

And while Brandy's—the bar in question, whose motto was, somewhat prophetically, "Where incredible friendships begin"—has long since closed, almost forty years later my parents are still going strong.

That first night, when he spotted her across the room, it didn't take long for my dad to work up the nerve to ask my mother to dance. This might not seem like such a grand gesture to anyone else, but while the current version of my dad is good at a wide range of things, dancing is certainly not one of them. To this day, he has a tendency to trip over pretty much anything in his path, so between that and the fact that he's more than a foot taller than my mom, I can hardly blame her for saying no. The idea of dancing with him must have seemed mildly terrifying.

But even after she'd politely refused, Dad remained undeterred, asking if he could drive her home instead. When she informed him that she was there with her roommate, he offered to take them both.

Outside their apartment, he asked Mom for her number.

She sized him up with a smile. "It's in the phone book."

This being Boston, there were countless O'Connors in the white pages, and so she never *really* expected him to call. But, of course, he did. The very next day.

Their first few dates were less than promising. He took her to a college hockey game, followed by a trip to the circus, and then a Red Sox game at Fenway Park, where she had to ask what the difference was between a ball and a strike. But despite her lack of sports knowledge, they continued to date casually for the next few months, seeing each other here and there, never really entirely serious, though interested all the same.

That spring, when Dad graduated from law school in the midst of a bad recession, he was only offered 2 jobs (despite having applied to 274 firms), and neither of them was in Boston. Even so, when he left for Chicago, there was no dramatic parting. He and Mom liked each other, sure. But they were young, and there were plenty of other people out there. This wasn't exactly the end of the world for either of them. It's simply what happens along the way.

For the next few years, they led their own lives. Dad paid his dues at a firm in Chicago, while Mom worked long hours as a cardiac nurse in Boston. They both moved on, dating other people, going out with their friends. But they also exchanged Christmas cards each year, keeping tabs on each other from afar.

Three years later, Mom was asked to attend a medical conference in Chicago. She'd never been there before, and the only person she knew in the city was my dad. So she wrote him a letter asking if he'd like to have dinner while she was in town, thinking they'd catch up as old friends, share a bottle of wine, and then return to their own separate lives.

But they say timing is everything, and maybe that's true. Perhaps it was the years between them, or maybe it was just the right moment, but when they saw each other that night, something changed for them both.

My dad still remembers exactly what she was wearing when she walked into the restaurant. My mom still remembers the look on his face.

Just like that, it was love at second sight. A year and a half later, they were engaged. And six months after that, married.

Life doesn't always give you second chances, but for my parents, that's all it took to make them see each other in a completely new light. It's funny to think about how many people have crossed your path, brushed by you in a bar, asked you to dance, and what might happen were you to meet them again down the road. After all, these things can happen in the most unlikely of places: an afternoon at a ball game, dinner with an old friend, or even a little bar in Boston, where at least one incredible friendship did indeed begin.

✳ ✳ ✳

Jennifer E. Smith is an editor at Random House, as well as the author of two young adult novels, *The Comeback Season* and *You Are Here*. She currently lives in New York City, just a short plane ride away from her parents, who are still pretty awesome.

hazel

by Rachel Fershleiser

MY MOTHER IS A RETIRED PUBLIC ELEMENTARY school teacher. She is sixty-three, chubby, and starting to gray. She favors quilted vests appliquéd with apples, alphabet letters, and happy hand-holding multicultural children. She likes to meet her girlfriends for coffee at the gym after her Sweatin' to Showtunes class and go bargain hunting at Filene's Basement. She belongs to book clubs at both the local public library and the reform Jewish synagogue, but she rarely reads past the first few chapters, showing up anyway for tea and cookies. In short, if asked to picture the life of a Brooklynite English teacher, you'd be just about spot-on.

Recently, at a United Federation of Teachers convention, the icebreakers for retirees included the question,

"Where were you when you found out we'd put a man on the moon?" Hazel Ellen Fershleiser was the only one who answered that she had been hitchhiking through Yugoslavia.

By the time she met my father, at the positively spinsterish age of twenty-eight, my mother had been to all the expected European backpacking countries, plus India, Nepal, Pakistan, Iran, Turkey, and the Soviet Union.

On her first tour, she'd traveled with a group. The van broke down often, leaving them to sleep at gas stations, and the driver was perpetually stoned. Convinced she could do better, she placed an ad in *The Village Voice* seeking a traveling companion. She heard from a college girl named Virginia who was planning to buy a car in Germany, drive it around until it was considered used, and bring it home without paying duty. The two tooled around in a brand-new convertible Karmann Ghia until they couldn't stand each other and Mom took off in the other direction, hitching to France with a guy who needed to find a special bike part.

She decided to spend the summer of '74 in Afghanistan after, during a brief previous visit, she'd been captivated by its primitiveness. Walking distance from the Kabul airport, a farmer whipped an ox to keep it walking in circles, lifting water from a well. The men working the fields wore sandals and robes and looked like a scene straight out of the Bible. It all seemed so different from the Long Island suburbs, where everyone loved modern conveniences, and no one could imagine living like their ancestors.

That spring her friend Marsha had married Jimmy, an exterminator. Because the summer was high season for insect eradication, he couldn't leave New York and encouraged the two women to travel on their own. Mom and Marsha knew they couldn't backpack safely through Afghanistan as just two girls, so they came up with a practical plan of action: pick up men as soon as possible upon arrival.

That Marsha was married didn't seem to factor into this at all; she was already having afternoon delight with a fellow teacher between the 3 PM bell and her husband's return from work.

They arrived in Kabul and headed straight for "the Street of Hippie Hotels." In the courtyard outside the biggest, they spotted four men with a round of beers, a map, and a VW bus. After ten minutes chatting up the German twenty-somethings, invitations had been made and the six agreed to meet the next morning to set off for Mazār-e Sharīf.

Overnight, one of the guys was hospitalized with hepatitis. They visited him in the '70s Afghani medical center, horrified by the hundred-degree heat, abundance of flies, and lack of ventilation. Eventually, he gave them the Deutschland-dude equivalent of "go on without me, save yourselves!" and they did. They lost another companion when the VW bus wouldn't start and its owner stayed behind awaiting a mechanic. By nightfall, four travelers climbed into the back of a stranger's pickup truck: Marsha and Jurgen, Hazel and Thomas.

Thomas was twenty-one to my mother's twenty-seven, slim and blond and pale. He looked, by his own description, like a shampoo commercial. His English was better than the little bit of German she'd learned from her own mother, who'd grown up in Danzig before the war. Marsha and Jurgen became a couple instantly, but Mom was shy. She'd just lost her virginity, at twenty-six, to the first guy she'd seriously dated.

The four would hike the desert all day, covering their hair and sometimes mouths with bandannas to keep out the dust. Every night they'd find a field or rock to settle down on and smoke the boys' hash pipe. Only once did they get caught; a small bribe quickly sent the policeman away.

They traveled to Bamyan to see the world's tallest Buddhas,

carved into a cliff high above the town. (Decades later, these ancient statues would be destroyed by the Taliban who considered them an affront to Islam.) Nights were spent in a series of cinder-block huts by the side of the road; it was called a hotel, but without window screens or plumbing, it clearly wasn't intended for Westerners. None of them had showered in a week. It wasn't until she heard the clerk ask Marsha and Jurgen how long they'd been married that my mother realized they'd be rooming boy–girl.

Alone in their bunker, Mom and Thomas talked for a long time, explaining their family histories and different upbringings. Then he leaned close and said, "You know, it's very hard for me to sleep in the same room with you if we can't do anything more." She was tired, curious, and on birth control pills. She said sure.

And that's how, not thirty years after the end of World War II, the son of a Nazi soldier and the daughter of a Jewish refugee ended up fucking, stoned, in a hut in Afghanistan, as Buddha looked down from above. My mother was awesome.

The fling lasted all summer, but that was it. Mom had a flight scheduled for the start of the school year. They exchanged addresses, they wrote letters. Thomas returned to the small town where he worked as a potter. By the time he came to visit New York two years later, he stayed on the couch of the apartment my parents shared. My father didn't know Mom had been more than friends with the long-haired European boy who told him Central Park was "far out." Years after, my parents returned the visit, staying on Thomas's fold-out couch with their five-year-old daughter. I wet the bed.

✳ ✳ ✳

Rachel Fershleiser is the co-creator of Six-Word Memoirs and the co-editor of the *New York Times* bestseller *Not Quite What I Was Planning* and three other books. She is a senior editor at the storytelling website SMITH Magazine and her writing has appeared in *The Village Voice, New York Press, Print, Los Angeles Times, National Post,* Salon.com, *Fray Quarterly,* and several amazing print and online publications you've never heard of. She lives in New York City, where she is the director of public programming at the non-profit Housing Works Bookstore Cafe.

andrei

by Alexandra Stieber

MY DAD ATE ICE CREAM FOR BREAKFAST. Bubble gum, mint chocolate chip, and rocky road replaced scrambled eggs, toast, and bacon. Jamoca Almond Fudge and chocolate peanut butter filled the bowl instead of cereal and oatmeal. Pancakes were trumped by the classic trio of chocolate, vanilla, and strawberry. For one entire month, my father woke up every morning and headed to Baskin-Robbins for breakfast, until he had tried all thirty-one flavors.

A big draw to ice cream lovers, the Baskin-Robbins signature thirty-one flavors represented more than a variety of palate-pleasing tastes to my father. Having moved to the United States as a Romanian immigrant in 1980, he left a country where everyday items with which I grew up, and of which I took advantage, were rare, cherished commodities. Chewing gum was so precious, it was traded on the playground as a form of currency. People waited for hours at local markets in Bucharest for basic necessities like bread and milk, frequently to find that supplies had run out once they had reached the front of the line. When the latest Beatles singles would hit the charts, scared but desperate teenagers would hole up in someone's cellar, with towels shoved under door frames to muffle sounds, simply to hear the harmonious melodies of the Fab Four. And the only ice cream flavors on the menu were chocolate and vanilla.

America, and its thirty-one flavors, represented an entirely new world to my father. He could walk down the street during the wee hours of the night without a curfew looming over his head. He could listen to any record from any band from any country, with the volume blasting at ungodly decibels until his eardrums rang and the neighbors complained. He could talk about politics or philosophy or religion without the fear of arrest. As he studied to become a doctor, he could specialize in any field, rather than being forced into a profession. He could drink a beer at two in the afternoon on a Tuesday. He could even eat ice cream for breakfast.

His first few days on American soil, my father was staying with a good friend in Chicago. With its notorious howling winds, blustery cold, and drifts of snow higher than some rooftops, Chicago greeted my father with a chilly hello that first morning in his new home. Yet not even the Windy City's subarctic temperatures and tundraesque wasteland of a winter landscape could quell my father's spirits. He awoke, bright-eyed and bushy-tailed (Romanians are a hairy people, after all), and headed into the great white wonder to scrounge up a classic American breakfast at a local diner his friend recommended. He had just begun to hunch over against the cold winds and forge down the street when a brightly lit, pink-adorned storefront caught his attention. A Baskin-Robbins ice cream parlor, this store was nothing like anything my father had ever laid eyes on before. Countertops gleamed in the fluorescent overhead lights, and the pink-and-white-checkered floor made him a little dizzy. But nothing overwhelmed him more than the sea of multicolored tubs of ice cream that spread before him in the several rows of display cases. A veritable rainbow of flavors, the ice cream beckoned my father with promises of creamy, sugary goodness. My dad pressed his hands and nose against the glass of the first display case, taking in all the many names of the different flavors, shocked to find words like *bubble gum* thrown into the mix. Rocky road, in particular, was a baffling concept. A classic American breakfast of eggs, toast, and bacon had become an afterthought; my father decided then and there it would be ice cream for breakfast instead.

In his excitement, and still in the European mind-set of ice cream scoops being the size of golf balls, my dad ordered five scoops of ice cream. The woman behind the counter cocked her head to one side and, looking at my dad dubiously, asked if he was certain he wanted five whole scoops of ice cream. Puzzled by her hesitation, my father insisted that, yes, he would indeed like five whole scoops. At this point, the woman must have noted my father's accent because, laughing, she balled up an example of a typical American serving of ice cream, and posed the question of whether or not my father wanted five of these one last time. He promptly reduced his order to two scoops.

From that day onward, my father stopped for breakfast at the ice cream parlor every morning until he had tried all thirty-one flavors. With each bite of pralines and cream, chocolate ribbon, and rainbow sherbet, the harsh memories my father had brought with him from Romania began to slowly melt away. In a span of a few short days, he had gone from a life where only two flavors existed to one with thirty-one distinct varieties, not to mention a plethora of top-pings. Ice cream stood for the countless possibilities that awaited him in his new life—a life he would gobble up with as much zeal and hunger as he did his ice cream breakfasts those first few days in America. While my dad has since expanded his ice cream repertoire to include the ranks of two lovely gentlemen named Ben and Jerry, as well as the sinful Häagen-Dazs Belgian dark chocolate, his happi-ness for all that a simple scoop of ice cream can bring remains the same, and, personally, I can never dip a spoon into a pint without thinking about him, the lessons he has taught me, and the deep ap-preciation he has given me for all things chocolate.

✳ ✳ ✳

A displaced Yankee proud of her Romanian heritage, Alexandra Stieber was born in New York City in 1984 but grew up in Atlanta, Georgia, where she currently lives and works in advertising.

jud and claudia

by Ryan Doherty

WALKING PAST THE SCIENCE BUILDING DURING COLLEGE, I would always interrupt whatever conversation was in play, point at the double glass doors, and tell people that was the exact spot where my parents met.

It was the legs of a pretty brunette—raised in the small home of a large immigrant family—that caught the boy's attention. He was a senior pre-med student who wore John Lennon frames, read Ezra Pound, listened to the Moody Blues, and maybe took himself a bit too seriously. He had even attended Woodstock, though his clothes remained on, and he only stayed through Canned Heat before hitchhiking back to small-town Rhode Island. She was a first-year chemistry graduate student, away for the first time after attending a college near her home, a home where her mother kept a garden full of tomatoes and basil out back. It was in chemistry class that he first noticed her legs.

They had just finished the final when they first got to talking. Although she warned him she was seeing a football player from Yale, she accepted his request for a date. She stood him up on the first date, and in a playful bit of jousting, he did the same on the second. The third attempt finally proved successful, and after walking through the Corcoran Gallery of Art they meandered back through nearby neighborhoods, ending up at his small apartment where he put Traffic's *The Low Spark of High Heeled Boys* on the record player. Eyeing his long hair and David Crosby mustache, she said, "I expected Jimi Hendrix."

It wasn't long before they fell in love, wearing bell-bottoms and drinking wine at graduate school parties. They spent their Fourth of July in '72 seeing the Stones at RFK Stadium. He would soon meet her sister, who would eye his shoulder-length brown hair and suede coattails with suspicion. He would even meet her father once, just months before he died too young of a brain aneurysm, after driving her home from school. While never spoken about, her protective father assumed she was dating the boy driving the yellow Beetle.

After the wedding they moved into an apartment across the river from campus, where she did research at the National Institutes of Health while he finished medical school. Later, she'd follow him to Philadelphia on the promise of a one-year commitment, where they would settle seemingly forever. They'd have one curly-haired boy during a snowstorm, wait a few happy years while they worked out the kinks of raising children, then have two more sons, one the year Joan Jett proclaimed her love for rock 'n' roll.

This boy—the middle one—would end up studying literature and seeking a career in the written word, a dream his father had once entertained, before being pressured into medicine by his parents. They would take this boy to see his first concert, again the Rolling Stones, which seemed lame to him then, but wonderful now. And when this boy became a man and needed to find more appropriate hobbies besides video games and baseball cards, he'd have his mother teach him how to make gnocchi and play boccie ball.

"A little knowledge is a dangerous thing," wrote their chemistry professor mockingly on top of the test they took the day they met. Thinking himself clever, my dad filled in the rest of the Alexander Pope quote, "Drink deep, or taste not the Pierian spring: There shallow draughts intoxicate the brain, And drinking largely sobers us again." Minutes later, just after scoring a sad 42 on that test, he met my mom, and what little knowledge he seemingly had on that day—his twenty-first birthday—was at least enough to win her.

There comes a time in young adulthood when you reassess your view on your parents; you stop seeing them in the kitchen preparing gravy or leaning in the dugout during Little League; you begin to see them as actual people, not there just for you, but for themselves and for each other. Once you get past your own selfishness, you realize that their decisions in life shouldn't necessarily be all about their children. You begin to understand that sometimes, these choices should be about themselves, and for whatever reason, parents separate and divorce and remarry, and that is all right, too. Because they were once as young as you are, with their whole lives ahead of them. And they chose each other and they chose to have children, and proudly sent one of them to the very same university where they first met, where I'd spend four years pointing to the doors of the science building, telling everyone in sight, "That's where my parents met."

✳✳✳

Ryan Doherty is an editor at Random House, who published this collection, which is the only reason he was allowed to write this drivel. He lives in Brooklyn, and definitely would have stuck around at Woodstock.

kathryn and phillipe

by Kathryn Borel

MY RELATIONSHIP WITH THE WORLD CHANGED when my father fell into a hole.

When fathers are around their daughters, they should be disallowed from doing three things: crying, vomiting, and falling into holes. It is in these activities that we realize that they are—like us—simply bags of skin filled with a complex kinetic mush, held upright with bones that are breakable and governed by a grayish-pinkish glob that will one day die.

It is one of the inherent flaws in any child's relationship with their parent: Their survival is reliant on the belief that parents can do anything, while their introduction to reality is reliant on the initial recognition that their parents are fallible.

I wasn't there when he fell into the hole. My mother called me from our large log cabin in the woods of Quebec on the infuriating satellite phone with a delay that made it seem as though she'd traveled back in time, as a lark, just so she could communicate with me from the Iron Age. ("Surprise! It's Mum! All this smelting is ravaging my complexion!") I was on the couch in my Toronto apartment, trouserless, working my way through a medium-sized pizza and contemplating breaking up with the Norwegian computer programmer I was dating.

"Lovey? It's krchhhtt krchhhtt—your father has had a small accident." My mother's voice was higher than usual. The change in octave precluded her claim that the accident was small.

My heart went thrashy and I sat up quickly, causing the plate of food on my chest to shift sideways. The pizza flopped onto the floor and splattered red sauce all over the place.

She described the sequence of events: My dad had been engaged in his springtime bout of ill-advised and underresearched woodland retirement activities—transplanting a proud-looking cedar tree he'd found deep in the woods to a spot closer to the house. While he was digging a pit to accommodate the root system, he'd hit a hard patch of dirt. When he kicked the shovel to bust through it, the earth caved in around him, causing him to lose his balance and topple over at a weird angle. His knees had always been weak—he was a marathoner—and the tendon in the right one snapped. After hearing his frightened shouting, my mother came running and slid him out of the hole with the help of a small plastic sled.

I asked if he could walk.

"With difficulty. But he has an appointment with the doctor next week. It's not a very invasive operation. Please don't worry."

Two months later, I flew home for a visit. As I deplaned, a little planet of anxiety plunked itself onto my sternum. How would my elegant Frenchman father be different? How bad was his limp? Would he have a cane with a duck head on top? How could he chase me around the house with a kitchen knife for mistaking a Burgundy for a Bordeaux with a cane?

Near the luggage carousel, I saw a flash of familiar peppery hair above the throng. I jumped in the air to make eye contact with the head. My father, still so handsome with his nut-brown eyes and fine jaw, saw me and waved an old golf putter in the air. I trotted over to them and found the pair—fair Mum and dark Dad (who was now leaning on the putter for support)—and wrapped my arms around them both, poking my nose into my father's shoulder desperately like some kind of demented fawn. Pulling back, I nervously scanned him for changes. Is it me or is his hair whiter? That brown thing on his temple—beauty mark or liver spot? Why is he wearing *sweatpants* in public?

Making sure to steady my voice, I tapped the putter and did what I do when I need to make impotent a big hard feeling.

"What's your handicap?" I said.

My mother laughed. In one fluid motion, my father took a few steps back, assumed a fencing stance, raised the putter and swiftly jabbed it into my belly. I coughed out a cough, and then a huge laugh. This was all going to be fine.

We walked quickly, though a bit clunkily, through the parking lot to his fast black European sports car. He handed me his sports cane and I placed it on my lap for safekeeping during the ride.

Once we were on the highway and my father was deftly weaving between the lanes, I annihilated the idea of him as an infirm. This was my goddamn *dad*. Teenage lothario, amateur boxer, poverty-stricken self-taught classical French cook who'd sailed through the ranks to become the youngest night chef in the history of the Georges V hotel in Paris. He was the man whose father had been instrumental in smuggling Jewish children out of France during World War II and then scraped together everything he had to move his young family to Canada to start anew.

Phillipe Borel lasered in on my mother, knew she was his destiny, corrected her quiche-making technique on their first date (she didn't blanch the bacon), five years later impregnated her with me out of wedlock, stoically and graciously abided the cruelty of her father (who called him his sin-in-law), and married her on a beautiful sail-boat when I was a year and a half old. He stopped cooking. He started collecting wines and managing hotels. He was asked to take over the Château Frontenac in Quebec City, the most photographed hotel in the world. He was awarded one of France's highest honors, the Chevalier de la legion d'honneur.

My father was a thousand feet tall and made of solid gold and we were driving along this highway in his race car at a thousand kilo-meters per hour and I was the idiot me for becoming mired in all this mortality stuff because he was going to live forever.

We arrived at the cabin two hours later. The sun was high in the sky and casting the trees and plants and water in a light that was grotesquely optimistic. The lake shimmered like oil in a hot pan that had been left on the stove by a careless cook. My mother unloaded the groceries from the trunk and I demanded my father bring me to the site of his accident so that I could better understand the me-chanics of his fall—to mock the dumb dirt and the dumb tree who'd been dumbly lucky enough to see this noble man in a rare moment of indignity. I grabbed his hand and laid it on my shoulder, for sup-port. My knees shook a little under his weight. He led me to the cedar and told me he'd named it The Crippler. Turning our backs to the woods, we walked up to the house while my father rattled off the names of the Burgundies he'd selected especially for me for dinner that night.

Inside, my mother was chopping food and pushing around pans on the stove. I went into the living room and settled onto the couch to read. Looking up from my book, I saw my father shuffling around at the top of the staircase that led to the basement and his cellar. He leaned his golf club on the railing and started down the wooden steps with an uneven thumping—a sort of *thu-thunk, thu-thunk.* Then there was a big thunk, a real THUNK, and a bellowing that went *oooohhhhhhpps,* and a crack and a crash, and then some defeated groaning. At the *oooohhhhhhpps,* I'd shot off the couch and run to the landing. He was at the bottom of the stairs, his body as curved as a shrimp's, perfectly still save for the gentle rise and fall of his shoulder. My heart charley-horsed.

My mother and I helped him to his feet. We lumbered back up the stairs and put him in his armchair. We did some knee-patting and hair-smoothing and general fussing. He sighed and said he was fine. His Lynx-point Siamese cat, Taomina, leapt onto his lap and began mincing around, searching for a comfortable spot. I was having insane thoughts: I had to laminate him, or find the largest pickling jar and store him in formaldehyde. Where was cryogenic technology? Wasn't Walt Disney still alive in some smoking ice vat underground? Couldn't we just do that to my funny, crazy, wise, wonderful dad? He was too rare to die. I wanted to put him under museum glass that would never break.

I realized I was standing there, slack-jawed from unreasonable scientific solutioneering, so I turned to him and asked if he wanted me to fetch the Burgundies. He gave me a list of four names.

Once downstairs, I hauled the wooden decoy panel off the wall to reveal the cellar door. My father had spent a few years smuggling attractive wooden wine crates out of the Château Frontenac and had a carpenter break them down, hot-glue and frame them. He was worried about intruders. (There were also two other decoy panels hanging on two adjacent walls, but they were ornamental. My father was also worried that the initial decoy looked too much like a decoy.)

Opening the door, I was hit with a cool blast and a familiar smell of earth and wet and mushrooms. I stepped inside and turned on the light. As I was poking around for the Burgundies, I ran my hand over some of the older bottles, their bodies gritty with compacted dust. I located my birthday bottle, a 1979 La Romanée my father had given to me in my late teens. It would be ready to drink in a few years. I scanned the other labels—a bottle of Taylor Fladgate port from 1945, a series of Madeiras from 1973, 1951, 1830. Eighteen thirty. I reeled at the idea of consuming a soul that had been around to witness the independence of Belgium, the rise and fall of disco, and also spaceships, all in one lifetime. There were pockets of the cellar that were empty, too. It was clear that since my father's retirement, my parents had not been taking lightly this business of honoring their collection. They were drinking. They were living. They were releasing this stuff from the glass and putting it inside of them in the name of sensuality and joy and occasional moderate tipsiness. The metaphor was all around me, whacking me in all the parts of my head like so many cast-iron frying pans: The wine is there to be drunk. Don't fear its disappearance. Enjoy it, stupid.

"Hey dear *daughter*," my father shouted from upstairs. He placed a long, liquid joke-emphasis on the *au*.

"What *is it*?" I shouted back.

"It is my desire to drink these bottles at some point tonight, not next year or the year after, hein?"

I located the four bottles he'd requested.

"Relax, old man. I'm coming."

✳ ✳ ✳

Kathryn Borel was born in Toronto in 1979. She has written and broadcast for many top-rated local and national programs on the Canadian Broadcasting Corporation's radio service, and is a founding producer of CBC Radio One's national arts and culture show, *Q*. She is the author of *Corked*, a critically acclaimed memoir about family, grief, France, and wine. Her print journalism has appeared in the *National Post, The Globe and Mail*, and the Guardian newspapers, among others.

astrid

by Ophira Eisenberg

WHEN PEOPLE ASK ME WHO MY comedy influences are I
have to cite my mother. On one hand, she has an infectious joie de vivre and is the life of the party, but behind
that is a surprisingly wickedly dark sense of humor that I
deeply admire and strive to emulate. No one can tell a
funny "my-school-got-bombed" story like my mom.

The majority of her life was spent as a mother. She
married in 1945 at the innocent age of sixteen and was
pregnant immediately. Five kids and almost thirty years
later I came along, which means she changed diapers on
and off for forty years. Forty years! Four decades of tod-
dlers wailing, teenagers sulking, and babysitters stealing
from the refrigerator. And trust me—the woman doesn't
even like kids that much. Maybe this is why.

She grew up in Nijmegen, Holland, during World War II. Nestled up against the German border, Nijmegen is the oldest city in the Netherlands and was also the first to fall into German hands when Holland was invaded in 1940. The Dutch became prisoners in their own homes, as the Nazis went door-to-door, confiscating anything made of brass or copper, and of course their radios. One day, without forewarning or questions, they took my mother's father away for five years. They were rationed food, allowed one egg a month, and forced to wash their hair with gasoline as it was the only thing available that would kill lice. I'm just saying it's impossible to complain to my mother about your boring job or the stress of the holidays.

The British liberated Nijmegen from German captivity in September 1944. My father, born and raised in what is now Israel but back then was still Palestine, joined the British army and was part of this liberation movement. Before proper camps could be set up in Nijmegen, families opened up their homes to these soldiers, offering a safe place to sleep, a shower, et cetera. This is how my parents met. Forget about Match.com or a blind date; back then all you had to do was say hello to the guy who was lying on your living-room floor.

My grandmother adored my dad because of his generosity, and by that I mean good-intentioned thievery. He'd sneak into the army's kitchen and scoop handfuls of coffee, sugar, and salt into the pockets of his uniform and then quickly walk over to their house and present these luxury gifts. The children, including my mother, would be given the task of picking out every last granule and bean between the lint and dirt in the pocket lining—a World War II form of flirting.

Naturally he fell in love with my mother, although I think she had her heart set on another soldier. You see, she was a real hot number, and is even to this day at the age of eighty-one. But my grandmother stepped in and told her that she had to marry this man. He'd already shown that he had a big heart and could provide for her. He'd steal for her, for God's sake—what more do you want? But beyond his slippery fingers and exotic good looks, my mother saw something else. He was her ticket out of war-torn Holland. Little did she know it was an economy pass to Palestine, where she would raise two kids and endure a further slew of historic wars, but at least they were different wars. Finally in the early 1950s, she declared that she'd had it and just wanted to move somewhere peaceful. In response, the family boarded a ship and sailed to Canada.

My mother, Astrid, grew up Catholic, and went to an all-girl school run by nuns. She recalls these nuns as mean, harsh, evil women whose only pleasure in life was to invent cruel and unusual ways to punish their students. Let's say you were caught whispering to a friend. Well, you'd get hit with a stick. I can't say for sure if this experience led her to embrace Judaism later in life, but I'm pretty sure it didn't hurt.

The curriculum sounded as archaic as the disciplinary methods. Instead of trigonometry, the girls took handcrafts and learned how to properly fold sheets and towels to organize a linen closet. My mother clearly got an A in that class, as her linen closet is so inhumanly perfect, it'll make you scream.

This one nun, the wickedest of the bunch, Sister McSuper Meany, really had it out for my mom. If she caught her daydreaming during a lesson, the nun would make her lift her skirt and kneel on the ground on her bare knees. It sounds uncomfortable but not torturous until you find out the ground was made up of a mixture of sharp gravel and slivery sawdust. Like I said, don't whine to my mom about how your trainer pushed you a little too hard at the gym.

On February 22, 1944, American planes heavily bombed Nijmegen. According to many historical accounts, the American pilots mistakenly thought they were bombing the German city of Kleve. Whoops! Don't worry—they issued an apology.

My mother remembers this day, similar to many other days in the sense that she heard the thunderous sound of explosions, but this time it was continuous and louder, as if the audio was looped seven or eight times. As a result the entire downtown area, including my mother's school, was completely destroyed. By total crazy luck, she wasn't at school that day. Instead, she was stuck at home taking care of her sick mother, an inconvenience that turned out to be a miracle.

The next morning, while doing her morning errands of finding food, she decided to ride her bicycle to the site of her school and view the wreckage. This was before TV. All she saw was a big pile of gray and black rubble. This was all that was left. It's a sobering thought to picture a young girl of fourteen or fifteen, propped up on her bike, awestruck, looking at this mess. She gazed around at what was the schoolyard. The trees that encircled it were strangely still standing.

Now, at this point in the story, my mom will get a little glint in her eye as she tells you about her next discovery. There, hanging in one of the trees, was Sister McSuper Meany, or as my mother would say it, "And there she was, the meanest one, hanging dead in a tree!" Then she'll throw her head back and laugh like this is the funniest punch line to a situation one could imagine. She'll punctuate it by adding, "Isn't life just so funny sometimes?" Then she'll go back to her handcrafts. The twisted poetic justice of it all. And because of this my mother is awesome.

✳ ✳ ✳

Selected as one of *New York Magazine*'s Top 10 Comics, Ophira Eisenberg has appeared on Comedy Central and VH1. She is a regular host for The Moth and has appeared on both their podcast and the *Audience Favorites* CD. Her writing has been published in four anthologies including *I Killed: True Stories of the Road from America's Top Comics* and *Heeb* magazine's *Sex, Drugs & Gefilte Fish*. She is also a regular contributor for *US Weekly*'s Fashion Police and a two-time MAC Award finalist for Best Female Comic.

don and corinne

by Rachel Sklar

IT ALMOST DIDN'T HAPPEN. But when you're a nineteen-year-old student nurse finishing her shift at 11:30 PM in 1962 and your blind date doesn't show up, you don't have much choice but to wait.

If you're a young twenty-three-year-old hotshot medical student, on the other hand, and your student-nurse blind date is nowhere to be seen, well then, you drive to her apartment, rouse her roommate, and demand to know where she is. Then you find out she's still waiting for you at the hospital, you goof, so you get back in your car and rescue her from having to walk home at midnight in downtown Toronto. Then you double down on a potentially awkward situation by going for cherry cheesecake. In Hamilton. An hour away.

"Come *on!*" I said to my mom. "What if you hated him?"

Good thing my mom wasn't as jaded as her daughter. That never occurred to her. She hopped in his car, and they sped off to Hamilton, Ontario, to find out if their friends Marshall and Linda were decent matchmakers. It was 3 AM when he dropped her off, so good thing they were.

A month later, they were engaged. Six months later, they were married. Forty-eight years later, they're still married. And I bet if I told them I was hopping into some dude's car at midnight to go have cheesecake in another city, they'd freak the hell out. (No offense, Dad, but even knowing the ending to the story, that still sounds creepy.)

I bet they'd also freak out if, a month into dating someone, I announced that we were getting married. ("What? You're marrying Weird Cheesecake Guy?") But everything was happening fast right then, so an engagement fit right in: My dad was graduating from medical school. He was buying his first car (a '62 Chevy Impala convertible with license plate D1379—and the *D* stood for "Doctor"). It only made sense to lock down a bride—especially when the bride looked like my mom. He was a young doctor, and had the license plate to prove it. It was time.

My parents are Don and Corinne Sklar. He's a psychiatrist and she's a lawyer, having gone back to school when her twins were nine and her baby, me, was just four. For most of my life, that was what they were: my parents, defined by having produced me, and my brother and sister. But before all that, they were just them, Young Don and Young Corinne, driving into the night for early-morning cheesecake, romance, and possibility.

A month into the "relationship" (sorry, I live in New York, a monthlong relationship definitely gets quotes), Young Don graduated from medical school, and Young Corinne turned twenty. His parents were throwing him a graduation party, so it was time to meet the family. Young Corinne joined the family for the graduation day ceremonies, and together they all drove to University of Toronto's Convocation Hall for the event, packed into his Chevy, with Young Corinne sitting primly in the front seat between Young Don and his father, with his mom, sister, cousin, and cousin's son squeezed into the backseat. (No seat belts, of course; if my parents caught me driving that way today, they'd hate Cheesecake Guy even more.)

My dad drove. My mom sat. No one said very much. From the backseat, very audibly, my Bubby Rose's voice stage-whispered to my dad's little sister: "Bernice! Talk to her!" Bernice hissed back: "I don't want to talk to her! *You* talk to her!" Poor Young Corinne was mortified. She was even more mortified later when she found out Young Don's buddy Marshall—one half of the couple who had set them up—had played what he thought was a hilarious joke: At the graduation party, he sidled up to Young Don's father, my Zaidy Max, clapped him on the back, and said: "Max! How do you like Don's girlfriend? Too bad she's not Jewish!" I am not sure if my Zaidy Max was drinking anything at the moment, but if he was, I imagine there might have been a spit-take. Max had come over from Poland to escape the war, my dad spoke only Yiddish for the first six years of his life, there may have been some Bund-type activities in the family (Yiddish socialist scholars, *you* know what I'm sayin'). Let's just say that marrying Jewish was a priority.

As it happened, Young Corinne *was* Jewish, very, as a matter of fact, and for the rest of their lives together let's just say only one of them ever showed a weakness for bacon. But despite that, Young Corinne found herself awkwardly blurting out Hebrew words in the middle of some dude's graduation party in order to prove her bona fides. Perhaps Young Don sensed that if there was going to be another "almost didn't happen" moment, this could have been it. So he took Young Corinne by the hand and discreetly led her upstairs, into his bedroom, and closed the door.

(And before I go on, it goes without saying that my parents would *not* be impressed at the thought of Cheesecake Guy pulling his wide-eyed young date into his bedroom while his parents threw a party downstairs. *Skeevy.*)

It gets skeevier: Passed out on the bed was one of Young Don's parents' friends, feeling unwell from the festivities and opting for a little nap. But before we go into teen-sex-comedy territory, I should stop teasing my dad already and reveal his purpose in luring my innocent young mother upstairs: He wanted to pin her.

No, not *that*. Pin her, old-school. There, in the shadow of a gently snoring partygoer and high above the noshing Jews downstairs, the brand-new doctor gave his brand-new girlfriend his fraternity pin.

"Wait. That was how you got engaged? A *pin*?"

Yes, said my mom. "We could't afford a diamond ring, so that was fine—we just figured we're gonna get married, which we did." I knew that was the voice of Young Corinne speaking, from the same place that made it seem perfectly reasonable to drive off to Hamilton at 12 AM for cheesecake. They knew they would be together. And they didn't need a license plate or a Hebrew test to prove it.

They were married five months later, in Ottawa where Young Corinne grew up. The bridesmaids wore pillbox hats. Afterward, they hopped into the Chevy—Young Mrs. Don was in a black wool suit trimmed with fox and very fancy, according to the write-up in the local Jewish paper—and drove through thick fog back to Toronto, the car filled with gifts and checks, to spend their first night together as a married couple and fly off to Nassau for their honeymoon the next morning. I asked my mom what they did when they got home. My mom demurred. My dad piped up: "You can tell her what we did, Corinne. We counted the checks to see if we could pay for the honeymoon or not!" Then my mom let slip that they overslept for their flight the next morning. I let out a snort. "It was very thick fog," my mom said. Uh-huh.

That's them, on the diving board at the hotel in Nassau, two crazy kids just starting a life together. They spent the first five years of their marriage just the two of them, getting the hang of married life and enjoying each other. It would have been cool to know them then, but maybe not: I probably would have told my mom to stay away from Cheesecake Guy. Luckily, he grew on me.

Rachel Sklar is a writer, editor, and social entrepreneur living in New York. As it turns out, she could probably stand to take dating advice from her parents.

panfilo and leonina

by Giulia Rozzi

MY PARENTS ARE SEXY. I'm not going to say they *were,* because I believe sexy never leaves your soul. Sure, their sexy
is less obvious than it used to be, what with their uniforms: my mother in her floral housecoat and my father
in whatever rejected T-shirt my sister or I thought we
threw away. Life may have caused them to dress themselves in aging ailments, complaints, and some bitterness
but at their core, Leo and Lea Rozzi are two sexy Italian
beasts.

My parents' prowess was most noticeable at weddings.
Every year there were at least one or two weddings my
parents attended. As two people who were too big of
workaholic martyrs to ever go on real dates, weddings
were my parents' big nights to get dolled up and do it up!
And since most of these weddings were Italian weddings,

they were often filled with many older stereotypical Italian guests (overweight women in slippers and overweight men with hair sprouting from their ears, nose, and wherever else hair can sprout from), causing my stunning parents to shine even brighter.

As a little girl I loved watching my mother get ready, especially for weddings. The way she'd widen her eyes and apply blue shadow and black mascara with a look of such importance. The way she'd brush, fluff, and adjust her hair until it lay with untouchable perfection (even though she sported the infamous short mom-do that, whether clean, dirty, messy, or styled, never seemed to change shape). The way she'd proudly admire her masterpiece by tilting her head right to left and left to right, modeling for the mirror, falling in love with her face with each raised-eyebrow-come-hither pose (a move I've since inherited).

And then, of course, there were her clothes. Oh, my mom's wardrobe dripped with such European sass that I imagine while on hangers the sleeves of her dresses held cigarettes up to their imaginary heads. Her outfits consisted of vibrantly patterned frocks, cleavage-embracing tops, and high-heeled somethings in every color under the sun. Her clothes always smelled clean and fresh from the bars of Dial soap she kept in her drawers and closet. I used to question why she kept many of her fashionable items in doubled plastic bags, until years later when those items became my one-of-a-kind vintage pieces, for which I appreciated her "obsessive storage methods."

For weddings, repeating an outfit was never an option for my mom. To her, it would be like wearing 1998's Oscar gown to 1999's SAG awards: Wouldn't everyone notice? So once or twice a year she purchased a new getup for her big night out. Usually she opted for fancy skirt-jacket combos. We're not talking *Working Girl* blazers; these were surprisingly sultry jackets with touches of classy bling.

My dad's vanity methods were slightly less calculated: shower, shave, and a squirt or two of Old Spice. I loved the way his cologne mixed with his never-fading scent of beer and BO. The three blended together to create a smell that was undeniably my daddy. He then put on either his blue suit or his brown suit depending on which one my mother delicately laid out for him.

And there they were, Sophia Loren and Marcello Mastroianni. I swear if you listened closely you'd hear hints of Italian accordions playing as they made their way to the door. But before they got into my dad's Cadillac, there were photos to be taken, lots and lots of photos. After all, it *was* prom night at the Rozzi house, and shots of the young couple needed to be taken at every possible angle, pose, and location. After a few pics, these photo shoots would become solo sessions of my mom. She'd lean against the wall or car, sit cross-legged and coy on the sofa, or my favorite: stand in front of the fireplace, back turned to the camera, looking over her shoulder.

After her *Vogue* spread was shot, my mom would spritz one last drop of Jean Naté on her neck and be ready to go. My sister and I would watch them from the window, waving good-bye as though we were the proud parents admiring how fast our little ones had grown. My parents would wave back, calling "*Arrivederci,*" my mom blowing us kisses, dramatically mouthing *I love you* as though she were going away to sea.

When they got home, my mom would be flushed from the one Sombrero she sipped on all night and my dad would be in denial that he was inebriated from the open bar. Back in the '80s it seemed dads were allowed to drink and drive, especially my dad, the superhero who was such a master driver he "*don't need no stupid seat belt.*" Such behaviors proved that the dozen or so saint cards my mom taped to my father's dashboard were in fact protective miracle workers.

My mom would hand us a plate of cookies and Baggies of Jordan Almonds to munch on while she'd recount the evenings' events in her deep Italian accent: "*So we walk in. Oh my God, everybody was looking at me! They ask where I get my dress. I say it's nothing special, you know try not to show off.*" (Insert mischievous smirk here.) "*Then we dance. Oh they had the most beautiful music playing: La Tarantella, La Campanella, The Chicken. Wow! Your father was dance so hard he sweat, what a donkey!*" (Insert my mom smacking my dad's arm here.) This old joke would make them both laugh: My dad would cackle like a car engine, and my mom would snicker from her still perfectly frosted lips.

When I got a little older and the invitations began to arrive that read "Mr. & Mrs. Leo Rozzi & family," I was ecstatic—my sister and I would finally be able to see my parents in sexy action. The getting-ready rituals were all the same: the hair, the makeup, the Old Spice, even the photo shoot, except this time I got to be in a few shots where I'd try to copy my mom's standing in front of the fireplace, back turned to the camera, looking over her shoulder pose. I must say for a seven-year-old, I was pretty saucy.

When we got to the weddings it was just as my mom described it: heads turned when she walked in and my dad would rule the dance floor as sweat ran through his shirt. And when I wrapped my arms around my dad to slow-dance I didn't even mind holding his soaking back because I knew it was soaked with joy.

✳ ✳ ✳

Giulia Rozzi is a New York City–based comedian, actress, and writer who has appeared on VH1, MTV, and CNN and has been published in *Playgirl*, *New York Press*, and the *Mortified* book series. She co-hosts the popular sex-themed storytelling show *Stripped Stories* and is the creator of TheMessage-Board.com Web series. More at giuliarozzi.com.

*Paste in your
parents here!*

_____

_____

_____

_____

_____

_____

_____

_____

_____

_____

_____

_____

_____

_____

_____

_____

_____

_____

_____

_____

_____

acknowledgments

Thanks to Hannah at Foundry, Ryan at Random House, Brinda Adhikari, Heidi Jones, Shephard Smith, Ahmed Fakhr, Clara Canepa, Leticia Frazao, Leslie Yazel, Janet Lee Toomey, Stephen Lenz, Kelly Reeves, Lindsay Weber, Nancy Kennedy, Zosia Bielski, Michele Norris, Amy Hatch, Susan Avery, Gillian Regan, Colleen Egan, Paul Malcolm, Natali Oliveri, Erin Scottberg, Julieanne Smolinski, Ellen Thompson, the Supleys, the Trincellitos, the Ponzos, the Stebels, the Webers, the Jeffersons, Joanne and David Weiss, and my sister, Ilana.

about the editor

ELIOT GLAZER is a writer, producer, and comedian living in
Brooklyn, New York. He is an editor at the Web humor site
Urlesque.com. Additionally, he performs regularly at the
Upright Citizens Brigade Theater, and has appeared on
NPR, ABC, and Fox News. More at eliotglazer.com.